FLORENCE OBSERVED

ANDRÉ BARRET

Translated from the French by Stephen Hardman

KAYE & WARD · LONDON

OXFORD UNIVERSITY PRESS · NEW YORK

This book is neither a specialized study of Florence, nor a mere descriptive guide, but something half-way between the two – one with its theory and the latter with its dull practicality – a presentation of Florence in which the intention has been to combine aesthetic sensibility *and* utility. The book is meant to be an invitation to a journey and, for those who have already made the journey, a collection of memories arranged in a kind of order. Since the discovery of Florence is a great adventure, the personal emotions of the individual must dominate; but a little guidance can be invaluable to the visitor who strolls round the city, while a modest background of factual information enriches both feelings and ideas, and memories.

'To enter Florence for the first time at the age of twenty and to say to oneself at every step, with a leaping heart, "Florence, I am in Florence", is one of those joys that do not occur twice in a lifetime.' Today, young people take to the road easily, and yet the joy so well described by André Suarès, that refined and rather neglected writer, has lost nothing of its intensity. Certainly, one cannot deny the lure of more distant lands which have suddenly become accessible, the instinctive attraction and curiosity aroused by the 'mystery' of societies that will soon have disappeared or the enthusiasm inspired by the revolutionary ideal of countries which symbolize revolt, liberty and progress only because they are not at the same stage of historical development as the West.

Young people dream of Turkey, Afghanistan or Nepal from a desire to 'opt out', or their idealism may draw them to China or Cuba. For a generation that is largely questioning our materialist civilization and seeking a new system of values, Florence offers a less mysterious and exotic adventure than these, but one which undoubtedly goes deeper: it offers the chance to get to know a city which, more than any other, bears witness to Man's taste and intelligence, his power to create beauty and to make what he has created blend with Nature. Florence is the living proof of the possibilities for happiness and nobility which exist even in a world that is unsure of itself.

The restrained balance and emotional sincerity of its

works of art offer a wisdom quite different from the hazy message of some remote esoteric cult, or the facile doctrine of political slogans. If the word 'wisdom' irritates some, who knows if they will not find it endowed with a new and even exciting meaning as they discover the genuine emotions of passion and anguish beneath the rational calm of the artists of the Quattrocento? These works, in which the human personality is asserted not consciously but by the sheer quality of the artist himself, reveal the artifice, the simplifications and excesses which nowadays often conceal ignorance, emptiness and, above all, a hollow vanity. Undoubtedly, a stay in Florence can help one to look at the world through new eyes. These old stones reflect hope.

Stendhal considered that it is the energy of the passions that engenders masterpieces and that, once the storm has subsided, everything becomes small, insignificant and distorted. Passion is a rare and demanding thing, but there are sham passions and the modern world has become adept at fabricating emotions for itself. The most trivial sensation, the slightest glimmer of an idea, assumes exaggerated proportions. How far we are today from the natural and extraordinarily rich outpouring of the Quattrocento! At that time to paint, to carve, to build, was not merely to 'express' oneself but to live. None of these artists would have thought of 'putting himself in his work', for he was already a part of his work by the sheer power of his genius.

The bombardment of ugly, vulgar images to which the modern eye is subjected has to a large extent destroyed the heritage of balance and harmony bequeathed by thousands of years of contact with Nature. Aesthetic judgement has become the privileged domain of dangerous specialists: enslaved by the pressure techniques of what is appropriately called a 'consumer' society, many people ask themselves not what they like, but what they ought to like. Beauty is something one learns, by an intimate familiarity with the beautiful. The most modest craftsman of the Renaissance, living as he did with fine buildings, paintings and sculptures all round him, looked, made judgements and developed passionate enthusiasms. If Florence is today one of the finest lessons in beauty that the world has to offer, it is because, from the twelfth to the seventeenth centuries, its inhabitants fervently wanted it to be so. When approving the plans for the Campanile, the Signoria ordered Giotto to execute them 'in such a manner as to surpass in magnificence, in height and in perfection, anything that the Romans and the Greeks could have done of this kind'. If the enthusiasm and collective awareness of the beautiful which inspired both Athens and Florence are to be reborn, a totally new system of ethical values must first be established.

The author hopes that he will be excused for his vehemence in adopting this point of view, but he sincerely believes that at the present time a certain kind of intellectualism and a quite widespread pretentiousness are doing untold damage to sensibility. Intoxication with barely understood ideas or words closes eyes and heart to the most simple and natural joys. On his last visit to Florence, in front of the doors of the Baptistry, the author passed a young man who, after reading the guide to his friends and looking briefly at Ghiberti's sculptures, proclaimed in a grave and imperious tone: 'You can say what you like, but that is not functional . . .'.

Despite the enthralling adventure experienced by the men of the Renaissance, it would be misleading to represent their epoch as a model of harmony. One must have the slightly blind enthusiasm of Goethe to see in Florence the image of justice, order and balance, and the proof of the wisdom of its rulers. Rivalries, intrigues, conspiracies and revolts lie at the heart of the history of this city which, from the thirteenth to the mid-sixteenth centuries, enjoyed only a few decades of peace. In the glorious years of the Quattrocento, people were tortured with red-hot irons and quartered on the public squares. The Republic, before being finally swept away by the Medici, had always been controlled by a few: only one inhabitant in a hundred played a part in political life, and even he was nearly always dependent on some wealthy family. Except for the blundering Commune that followed the Ciompi revolt, the government remained in the hands of a capitalist oligarchy which humoured the people with demagogic measures while using it to strengthen its own power. And yet, during this period when, as Machiavelli wrote, 'all states are violent and legitimate power does not exist', both Florence and Venice, thanks to their commercial prosperity, experienced a uniquely privileged adventure.

Two or three thousand citizens aware of their rights and duties, out of a population of nearly one hundred thousand, seems little enough and yet they represented a force of extraordinary richness. If the democratic functioning of the councils was to be rapidly thwarted by the most powerful and ambitious, these institutions none the less reflected a new spirit: the rights of the individual had finally been asserted against those of the Prince or the Church.

The wealthy merchants and bankers had replaced the nobles as the rulers of the city. They acquired a passion for knowledge and beauty, they had the feeling of belonging to a time when everything was possible. Their exalted faith radiated over the whole population. A certain spirit of independence had always been traditional in Florence – as befitted the intelligence, refinement and pride of these descendants of the Etruscans. At the end of the thirteenth century the envoy of the first Habsburg emperor, who had just been elected, was ill received 'because never has the Commune of Florence sworn fealty to the emperor through any intermediary and because it has always lived and always been free'. Throughout the vicissitudes of internal strife, the Florentines who joined with either Pope or Emperor always remained loyal to the principle of the freedom of their city, seeking for it both glory and prosperity.

It must be admitted that a certain amount of enlightened capitalism was an essential element in the awakening and blossoming of the Renaissance! Pico della Mirandola and Leon Battista Alberti were two exceptional geniuses, but the same perfectionist aspirations were to be found in the majority of the bankers and rich merchants. The 'return to Antiquity', though one of the characteristic features of the period, did not play the determining role with which it is sometimes attributed; the ancients were, by their example, stimulating masters, they were studied and admired, but the curiosity and exuberance which brought about this wealth of artistic creation would have been alien to them. It is difficult to explain precisely why, in the history of humanity, these intervals of light suddenly appear. They are not simply the product of chance. After centuries of submission and gloom, a change of economic and social equilibrium had made possible the outpouring of long-suppressed forces and passions: the world of the Renaissance, impatient for discovery and novelty, was succeeding the Middle Ages.

In the history of art the beginning of the Quattrocento is one of those periods when an ideal balance seems to have been established between the natural, instinctive forces in Man and the forces of knowledge, leading to the creation of the most noble and sincere works of art. These artists had preserved their simplicity intact. A peasant vigour and a craftsman's modesty nurtured works of brilliance and vitality. The blossoming of these men was a natural process: ideas uplifted them, but did not dominate them. In their art there was the joy of discovery, but as yet no conscious intention. The Renaissance had the freshness and beauty of adolescence.

In contrast with the convulsive political history of Florence from the thirteenth to the sixteenth centuries – with its conspiracies, its factions and its revolts – the art of these three hundred years shows an admirable continuity from Duccio to Michelangelo. It seems almost as if these artists were holding one another by the hand, each absorbing training and experience from his predecessor, then living his own personal adventure before handing on in his turn the knowledge he had acquired and the discoveries he had made. In the sixteenth century this grace became distorted. Theories, a taste for artifice, turgidity and stylization appeared and at the same time the imitation of Antiquity grew more slavish. The quiet harmony and slightly austere elegance that had seemed natural to Florence were no longer acceptable. Rome became the capital of the Baroque and Florence immured itself in its memories. Michelangelo, with his taste for the ancient and the gigantic, is sometimes held responsible for this abrupt decline. In fact, the end of the reign of Lorenzo de' Medici had marked the beginning of a grave crisis and the Renaissance had seen the enthusiasm of the first humanists turn to disillusionment: after the vigour of Donatello, the melancholy of Botticelli; after the naïve faith of Fra Angelico, the imprecations of Savonarola.

But it was certainly Michelangelo, described by Rodin as 'the most powerful genius of modern times', who in the glorious twilight of Florence was to set art on its new path of 'personal expression', of an acute consciousness of individuality, after centuries of anonymity and self-effacement. For thousands of years the artist had kept his personality out of his art, which had been the expression of a faith, a system of knowledge and a tradition. This was true even of Giotto and Donatello. The time came when, in art as in other spheres, Man was to reveal his yearning for power, his desire to express himself, for himself and through himself, thereby bringing about the destruction of the harmony between Man and Nature. Yet, even if this need for personal expression imperilled the sincerity and purity of art, which was now at the mercy of the excesses of emotion and intention, it was part of the destiny of Man and, with him, was embarking on an uncertain but thrilling venture.

Florence has kept the look of its most splendid years and its later additions retire discreetly into the background. It is a dignified and reserved city; its rather austere grace tends to make one forget the extraordinary innovating force that gave it life. It was in Florence that the West saw the first cathedral dome erected and the first nude carved; it was here that artists discovered the laws of perspective, that the first library was opened to the public, and that the first opera was performed. In Florence modern thought was born: poetry with Dante, humanism with Petrarch, criticism with Boccaccio, and political science with Machiavelli. Tuscan was Europe's first modern language and eventually became modern Italian; even in the nineteenth century the great poet Manzoni came, as he himself said, 'to bathe' his 'language in the waters of the Arno'. The genius of Florence is not universal, for it reflects its own character, its quality of balance and restraint. It has been said that this city was the capital of the Elements of Euclid and that, like its last great man, Galileo, it was a little too perfect, lacking the sense of the infinite and the tragic. Admittedly, Florence is above all a city of intelligence and harmony. Yet who has expressed the anguish of the human condition more strikingly than its two most illustrious artists, Leonardo da Vinci and Michelangelo? These two geniuses impelled by mighty ambitions, one for knowledge, the other for artistic creation, pushed themselves through solitude and suffering up to the limits of Man.

If, when one is twenty, Florence is a marvellous discovery, it remains throughout life an ideal friend to those who can return to the city from time to time. By its grace and beauty it illumines and comforts; perhaps because it is the epitome of equilibrium and intelligence, it makes one take one's bearings: the emotions and reflections it inspires measure the time and distance which each of us has travelled. Anyone who has the good fortune to live in Florence and who learns to know it intimately is entranced by the quality of mind and heart of its inhabitants. It is the most refined and sensitive city in Italy, and also one of the most generous in its social and political intentions. Florence has not forgotten its glorious past and yet, enterprising and active, it lives in the present. That said, though one may find the familiarity with which it treats its works of art appealing, one is inclined to reproach the city for insulting them with its noise and clutter. The all-powerful cult of the motor car and the reluctance of individuals to give way to the general good have so far prevented certain essential decisions from being taken: for example, prohibiting traffic in the centre of the city, and clearing squares such as SS. Annunziata and Santo Spirito of their unsightly car parks.

Finally, without wishing to discriminate against tourists, one cannot help regretting that Florence, burdened as it is with those who seem to come to life mainly during shopping hours, does not always have the public it deserves. Of course, one cannot insist that visitors have a 'certificate of sensibility'! In a world in which cultural education has not yet been fully accepted, visitors will sometimes pay their tribute of admiration uncouthly, though always with goodwill.

Twenty centuries separate the Athens of Pericles and the Florence of Cosimo de' Medici . . . civilizations are never in a hurry. When, then, will beauty triumph once more? Perhaps in a thousand years? In the meantime, if you feel so inclined, let us set off together to visit Florence.

A.B.

Simonetta Vespucci by Piero di Cosimo.

Thus spake the Lord: 'We have given you, Adam, neither a fixed place, nor an aspect of your own, nor any special privilege, so that the place, the aspect and the privileges that you desire you may obtain and preserve yourself according to your own inclinations. The clearly defined nature of the others is a prisoner of the laws that we have proclaimed. But you, who are not a prisoner of any constraint, you will determine your nature according to your own free will to which I have entrusted you. I have put you amidst the world so that from there you can better perceive all that is in the world. We have made you neither heavenly nor earthly, neither mortal nor immortal, so that, as the free and sovereign modeller and sculptor of yourself, you can carve yourself in the shape that you choose. You can degenerate and fall to the lower beings who are the animals; you can, if you so decide, regenerate yourself and climb towards the higher beings who are divine.'

PICO DELLA MIRANDOLA
Discourse on the dignity of Man (1486)

16

1

PONTE VECCHIO – PIAZZALE MICHELANGELO – PIAZZA DELLA SIGNORIA – PALAZZO VECCHIO – DUOMO – BAPTISTRY – OPERA DEL DUOMO.

The sight of Florence is dazzling at first, but as the eye becomes accustomed to it, gaiety fills the heart.

Take a stroll along the Arno, which divides the city and provides its most glorious perspective. Florence has always been in danger of floods from this river which, although very low in the summer, can become torrential. In the Middle Ages, as in the time of its greatest splendour, sudden floods devastated the city. Buildings and masterpieces of art had to be rescued from the mud in the floods of November 1966. Immediately the world felt united, aware that here was a supreme testimony to the greatness of Man and to his power to create beauty.

THE PONTE SANTA TRINITA *was built by Bartolomeo Ammannati from 1566 to 1569. With its two slender pillars and its three arches of high curvature, it is a striking combination of strength and lightness. At the ends of the bridge, which used to be a place of public entertainment and where plays were performed, four seventeenth-century marble statues represent the seasons. The bridge was destroyed in August 1944 by the retreating German army, but was faithfully reconstructed in 1957. Its graceful lines were always dear to the hearts of Florentines.*

The famous PONTE VECCHIO *('Old Bridge') deserves its name, for it dates from the fourteenth century. Like Florence itself, it is a delicious mixture of rustic simplicity and elegance. Rebuilt after the disastrous floods of 1333, it has since been preserved intact.*
At one time the butchers' stalls stood here; the situation had its advantages, for the butchers used to throw their waste meat into the Arno. In the sixteenth century, no doubt sensitive to the smell, Cosimo I decreed that the butchers must make way for the goldsmiths and jewellers, who have remained here ever since, adorning the bridge with their tempting wares. Cosimo I also commissioned Vasari, his Jack of all trades, to build a long corridor, above the shops, which passed through the Uffizi, linking his residence, the Palazzo Pitti, with the seat of government, the Palazzo Vecchio.
Cosimo I (1519–1574), who became the first grand duke of Tuscany, must not be confused with Cosimo the Elder (1389–1464). The hundred and thirty years separating their births represent the most glorious epoch of Florence. The first Medici to reign officially over the city, Cosimo I was an active and intelligent prince who strove to emulate the glory of his great-grand-cousin, Lorenzo the Magnificent; but he did not have Lorenzo's genius and Florence itself had lost its driving force.
In revenge for the abandonment of his betrothed, Buondelmonte dei Buondelmonti was murdered by the outraged family on Easter Sunday 1215 at the end of the Ponte Vecchio, an act that was to unleash the bloody conflict between 'Guelphs' and 'Ghibellines'. Originally signifying the two parties that supported the rival candidates for the Holy Roman Empire, Otto of Welf and Frederick II of Hohenstaufen, these terms rapidly came to mean the champions of the Pope and the Emperor, respectively.
For a long time the Ghibellines were the more powerful, then the Guelph party established its supremacy. These confrontations, which lasted more than a hundred years with fluctuating fortunes, were provoked largely by rivalries between great families. On the whole, the rich merchants and craftsmen were Guelphs, supporting the Pope and, above all, asserting the independence of their city in the face of the ambitions of the Emperor.

One can spend hours on the Ponte Vecchio. This bridge, a wonderful setting for a parade, is an ideal place to watch the people of Florence walking by in a colourful procession. You should go there between nine and ten in the morning; the tourists have not yet gathered in front of the little shops of the silversmiths and jewellers, and you can see the Florentines hurrying to work. A painter has already set up his easel, the first groups are forming, two smartly dressed *carabinieri* walk up and down, a pedlar blows soap-bubbles as he pushes his bicycle. . . . There are some beautiful Florentine women among the early-risers, tall and slender with fine necks and lovely faces. The Florentine women are reputed to be the most elegant in Italy; their favourite colours are browns and ochres of every shade, dark red and violet.

The Ponte Vecchio is the busiest and most direct route between two very old and lively quarters of the city: on the right bank, the Piazza della Signoria district; on the left bank, known as the 'Oltrarno', the junction of roads on the Via Guicciardini, which leads off from the bridge. As one sets foot on the paving-stones of the Oltrarno, one suddenly seems to rediscover the passions of the Middle Ages and the Renaissance. Modern shops occupy the ground floors, but the houses have preserved their old nobility and mystery; carefully rebuilt after the devastations of the war, those overlooking the Arno have recovered something of their picturesqueness. Palaces of the thirteenth and fourteenth centuries, and of the Renaissance, line the Via de' Bardi, which leads to the embankments and the slope rising up to the Piazzale Michelangelo. From this square there is a marvellous panorama of this city of pink, green and white. Two buildings dominate the city: the Palazzo Vecchio, firm in its lines and utterly medieval; and the cathedral, a beautiful example of the harmony of Renaissance architecture.

On the way to the Piazza della Signoria you will be able to observe the dignity of the older Florentine women and the gracefulness of the younger ones, and the old men with their mischievous eyes, half townsmen, half peasants.

Active, intelligent and shrewd, the Florentines are

naturally reserved with foreigners. Stendhal complained of the Florentine: 'His keen, piercing eyes seem more inclined to judge you than to like you.'

Certainly, the Florentines have a caustic wit and, sometimes, a ribald tongue. While they have retained the spirit of simplicity and equality that characterized their ancestors, they also seem to possess a feeling of natural superiority. To be born in the most beautiful city in the world gives them a right to be proud; after all, Giotto, Donatello and Michelangelo were their forefathers.

The great events in the history of Florence took place on the Piazza della Signoria or in the palace that stands on this square, the Palazzo Vecchio, which boldly thrusts skywards the bayonet of its tower, ninety-four metres high.

In the thirteenth century this part of the city, which lay over the ruins of the ancient Roman theatre, was occupied by the dwellings of the powerful Ghibelline family of the Uberti, who belonged to the imperial nobility. Since Otto I (962), the Emperors of the Holy Roman Empire, continuing the Carolingian tradition, had had themselves crowned kings of Italy. At first supporters of the Papacy, they soon became its rivals in the peninsula. To safeguard their autonomy, the duchies and cities turned to the Holy See, whose suzerainty was more gentle. The Emperors Henry IV, Frederick Barbarossa and Frederick II had engaged in some terrible quarrels with the Sovereign Pontiff. After quite a long period of success and the victory over the Guelph nobility at Montaperti in 1260, the Emperor's supporters in Florence were finally defeated by the Pope's party. The houses of the Uberti were demolished and the boundaries of the present square were thus laid out. It was then decided to build for the new government of the Commune a palace worthy of its power. The construction of the palace, which took from 1299 to 1314, was entrusted to the great architect Arnolfo di Cambio, who also made the plans for the Cathedral and for Orsanmichele. In this palace the Gothic style, imported from France by the Cistercians, finds a sober and original expression. As soon as it was completed the *Signoria* or governing committee was installed there. Its nine members, at first called *priori*, then *signori*, met for two months every year; they each lived in a palace apartment but took their meals at the same table, and they were to devote all their time to public affairs. However, the real power belonged to the *Gonfaloniere di Giustizia* (Gonfalonier of Justice) and to two councils: the council of the people and that of the Commune, which in the most serious matters were themselves subordinate to another council, the *balia*, appointed by the assembly of the people.

The military mass of the Palazzo Vecchio is a reminder of the turbulence of the period. As the factions quarrelled for power, plots and insurrections were frequent. The

TAXI

bitter struggles between Guelphs and Ghibellines were followed by bloody conflicts between 'Black' and 'White' Guelphs. Dante, when elected a *priore* of the Signoria, tried to reconcile the 'Whites' who, like himself, advocated the independence of Florence from Rome, and the 'Blacks', the intransigent champions of the Pope. The arrival of Charles of Valois in the city resulted in the proscription of the 'Whites' in 1301. Dante was banished from Florence and threatened with burning at the stake. Although it represented a new spirit for the period, the 'democratic Commune' remained in the control of a few. For a time the *Arti Maggiori*, the seven richest guilds, found themselves challenged for power by the *Arti Minori*, the less wealthy guilds.

The Black Death of 1348 killed half of the city's population. By the end of the fourteenth century Florence was ripe for the oligarchy of a few powerful families, among whom the Medici, extremely prosperous bankers and ambitious politicians, quickly established their supremacy.

In 1478 the Piazza della Signoria witnessed the climax of the conspiracy hatched by the Pazzi family, the rivals of the Medici. Giuliano and Lorenzo de' Medici were to be assassinated in the Cathedral. Only Lorenzo escaped death, whereupon he imposed his rule over the city. On Lorenzo's death in 1492 power was seized by Savonarola, the tempestuous Dominican who constantly fulminated against the unworthiness of the clergy and the corruption of the Papacy, preaching a return to spiritual values and to political independence. He ruled for four years, inspiring a theocratic republic with a constitution modelled on that of Venice. In 1497 he organized a 'bonfire of vanities' on the square, burning masks, wigs, dice, musical instruments, books of poetry and paintings of profane subjects. The people showed their fickleness a year later when, at the very same place, now marked with a bronze medallion, the stake was erected at which Savonarola himself was burnt.

In the fifteenth and sixteenth centuries the square was used for public festivals, tournaments and even bullfights. Today it is still the scene of big political demonstrations. Several times a year the inhabitants, in costume, play *calcio*, a game which was the popular sport of the Renaissance and the forerunner of modern soccer.

The refinement of the palace interior offers a striking contrast. In the courtyard, elegantly decorated with stuccoes by Michelozzo, Verrocchio's bronze statuette, *The Child with the Dolphin*, placed on the fountain, is a masterpiece of Florentine art. The Grand Council Chamber, the delightful *studiolo* (the study of Francesco I, second grand duke of Tuscany), the sumptuous apartments of Leo X, the first Medici Pope, and Cosimo I are very typical of the decorative style of the sixteenth century; they are mainly the work of Vasari, an artist without much character but whose writings are an invaluable source of information on the great artists of the Renaissance.

One must go to the Room of Maps and see the contours and colouring of the countries and continents to understand the wonderful adventure of the imagination that was made possible by the great navigators' discovery of the world.

In Florence the glorious years of the Renaissance and the tumultuous passion for liberty came to an end with Cosimo I, who secured power in 1537. If the first grand duke of Florence deprived his subjects of the excitements

of political life, he encouraged those of artistic life, for he wanted to see his people living amid masterpieces. Today those masterpieces still stand on the public square, where people can move among them with complete freedom.

The Loggia dei Lanzi, built at the end of the fourteenth century, was at first a place of assembly on rainy days, then the guardhouse of the *lanzi*, the unpopular lansquenets or mercenaries of Cosimo I. It is adorned with numerous ancient and Renaissance statues, including two marble groups by Giambologna, *The Rape of the Sabines* and *Hercules and the Centaur Nessus*, and Cellini's famous *Perseus*.

Near the palace entrance are statues of republican inspiration: the *David* which revealed the genius of Michelangelo has been replaced by a copy; the *Marzocco*, the fierce lion by Donatello, embodies the pride and independence of the Florentine people; the group *Judith and Holofernes*, also by Donatello, was erected after the first expulsion of the Medici (1460), as a warning to tyrants.

On the other side of the entrance to the Palazzo Vecchio a rather ugly statue by Bandinelli, *Hercules slaying Cacus* (1534), proves that the Renaissance, especially towards the end, did not produce only masterpieces.

MERCURY, *one of the four bronze statuettes adorning the pedestal of the 'Perseus' by* BENVENUTO CELLINI *(1500–1571).*

PERSEUS. BENVENUTO CELLINI

THE FOUNTAIN OF NEPTUNE. *The bronze fauns and nymphs, gracefully arranged on the edges of the basin, are the expression of a refined, sensuous art; they are the work of Buontalenti and Giambologna; this latter artist was also responsible for the fine equestrian statue of Cosimo I in the centre of the square.*
The Fountain of Neptune was commissioned on the occasion of the wedding of Joan, daughter of the Emperor, with the future grand duke Francesco I, son of Cosimo I. This marriage, though bringing glory to the Medici, confirmed the vassalage of the grand duchy.
The fountain was executed from 1560 to 1575 under the supervision of BARTOLOMEO AMMANNATI, *who was responsible for the graceless statue in its centre. Every time Michelangelo passed near the 'Neptune' he is supposed to have said: 'Ammannati! Ammannati! what beautiful marble you have spoilt. . . .' The Florentines mockingly call it 'il Biancone' ('the white thing').*

The cupola of the Duomo or cathedral is an architectural *tour de force*, rising above Florence like a crown of glory to the Renaissance. It was the work of the greatest of the Florentine architects, Filippo Brunelleschi. The cathedral was begun in 1296 by Arnolfo di Cambio, who was commissioned to 'build the highest, the most sumptuous and most magnificent church that the human mind can devise and that human hands can execute'.

After his death (1302) the building work was supervised by Giotto (1334–1337), who was responsible in particular for the plans of the admirable Campanile or Bell-tower. After Giotto the overseers were Andrea Pisano (1337–1348) and Francesco Talenti (1349–1369). Talenti gave the cathedral its new dimensions (a hundred and fifty metres long, ninety metres wide at the transept), thus making it the largest church in Italy. Brunelleschi won a competition held to find a design for the cupola originally intended by Arnolfo. His design was the most beautiful and the most daring: an octagonal cupola, comprising double concentric domes, constructed on a principle of incurvation and by a technique that rendered large frameworks and scaffoldings unnecessary.

Contemplating the Duomo before undertaking the cupola of St Peter's in Rome, the proud Michelangelo is supposed to have said: 'I shall give it a bigger sister, but will mine be as beautiful?'

TAXI

The origins of the BAPTISTRY OF ST JOHN *are shrouded in legend; it is difficult to establish the date of its construction, which belongs somewhere between the sixth and eleventh centuries. It is an octagonal edifice with a pyramidal roof, like a huge marble tent. Its elegant proportions and the freshness of its decoration, with the alternating white and dark green marble characteristic of Florence, mark the continuity between Romanesque art and that of the Renaissance.*
Dante was baptized here, like many thousands of Florentines. The heart of old Christian Florence, the interior of the Baptistry affirms the Romano-medieval character of the building. On the paving and the walls one finds the same graceful geometric interplay of white and green marble.
The cupola is covered with magnificent mosaics in the Ravenna tradition, though of much later date (thirteenth and fourteenth centuries); the mosaics are the work of Venetian and Roman craftsmen and their Florentine pupils, one of whom, Cimabue, after assimilating the Byzantine tradition, was to become the great precursor of Florentine painting.
The Baptistry contains two of Donatello's finest works: the striking wooden statue of the 'Repentant Magdalene' and the tomb of an anti-Pope prematurely named John XXIII, whose election was rapidly quashed in spite of Cosimo the Elder's patronage.

Michelangelo is also said to have declared that the doors of the Baptistry were worthy to be the gates of Paradise. The oldest is the work of Andrea Pisano; the two others are by Ghiberti who, for this work that occupied him for nearly thirty years, found himself preferred to some famous rivals – Brunelleschi, Donatello and Jacopo della Quercia.

This beautiful series of gilt-bronze panels, which thus took over a century to complete (1330 to 1452), enables one to trace the evolution of Florentine art, from the Gothic hieratic style of the first figures of Pisano to the quest for movement and grace which, in the middle of the Quattrocento, foreshadowed the Mannerism of the sixteenth century.

---

p. 30
Second door by GHIBERTI. *Above the door,* THE BAPTISM OF CHRIST BY ST JOHN, *by* SANSOVINO.

p. 31
right *Detail of the door of* ANDREA PISANO. BAPTISM OF CHRIST BY ST JOHN BAPTIST.
below *Detail of the second door by* GHIBERTI. ESAU RENOUNCES HIS RIGHTS OF PRIMOGENITURE.

Our modern artistic sensibility makes us forget that, in the great periods of art, architecture and sculpture were much more important than painting, the domain of individual expression.

In the evolution of architecture and sculpture in Tuscany, the republic of Pisa enjoyed pre-eminence from the eleventh to the fourteenth centuries. For three hundred years Pisa was a flourishing city; it was much more enterprising than Florence, by which it was to be politically subjugated only in 1405, after having become the victim of another rival, Genoa, in 1284. Dante, who called his Florentine fellow citizens *'gente avara, invidiosa, superba'* ('a miserly, envious and haughty people'), also said that the Pisans regarded them as 'a wild herd from the mountains'. The Pisans, good sailors who controlled the Tyrrhenian Sea, had seen something of the world: they had fought the Saracens in Spain, defeated the Emir of Egypt and taken part in the Crusades in large numbers.

The marble decoration of black and white horizontal bands which is peculiar to Tuscany and appeared in Florence in the eleventh century, in the Baptistry and at San Miniato, probably originated in Oriental stylistic elements to which the clear, rigorous Pisan mind gave a new order. In sculpture, Pisa established new forms of expression through the works of some very great artists.

Niccolò Pisano, born around 1220, occupies an important place in the history of Italian art. In his works Romanesque sculpture suddenly acquired a strange power. His pupil Arnolfo di Cambio was to be the architect responsible for the great Gothic monuments of Florence; the Palazzo Vecchio, the plan of the cathedral and almost certainly that of Santa Croce. His son, Giovanni Pisano, an original personality, worked on the façade of Siena Cathedral and on the baptistry at Pisa; the expressive power of his statues was to be equalled only by the frescoes of Giotto, whom he doubtless influenced, being some fifteen years his elder.

Andrea de Pontedera, who became Andrea Pisano, was also a Pisan but certainly did not possess the same dramatic vigour. In the bas-reliefs on the first door of the Baptistry, as in the admirable medallions of the Campanile, one discerns the softening influence of the Gothic art of the Ile-de-France. Yet his work displays the integrity, strength and joyousness that inspired the artists of the early fourteenth century. This sincere naturalism was to influence the great sculptors of Florence and remain the basis of their art. The perfection of form in Classical Greek statuary, and of expression and movement in certain Hellenistic works, was not to be rediscovered until the second half of the Quattrocento.

The Campanile, built to house the bells of the cathedral, is an edifice of surprising grace and lightness, despite its height of eighty-four metres. Its square plan is of great simplicity and, in its decoration of polychrome marble, the traditional green of Prato and white of Carrara are enhanced, as on the exterior of the cathedral, by the delicate pink of Maremma. Giotto prepared the plans in 1334 at the request of the Signoria which, in approving them, ordered that the Campanile must be built 'in such a manner as to surpass in magnificence, in height and in perfection, anything that the Romans and the Greeks could have done of this kind'. Such were the aspirations of the ambitious city.
After Giotto's death the construction of the Campanile, which lasted from 1334 to 1387, was directed first by Andrea Pisano, then by Francesco Talenti. The two series of bas-reliefs which run in a band across its lower part are justly famous. The twenty-eight hexagonal medallions are copies of those carved by Andrea Pisano, probably from drawings by Giotto (the originals are in the Museo dell' Opera del Duomo). In the form of mythological scenes or allegorical symbols, they represent Man at work, in a veritable encyclopaedia of human labour and Man's progress since his creation.

p. 32
STONE MEDALLIONS *by* GIOTTO *and* ANDREA PISANO. *These medallions, now in a room of the Museo dell'Opera del Duomo, once adorned the Campanile, where they have been replaced by copies. From top to bottom: 'Medicine or Pottery', 'Jubal in his tent, surrounded by his herd', 'The Drunkenness of Noah' and 'Work in the Fields'. The Museo dell'Opera del Duomo contains an outstanding selection of sculptures of the golden age of the Quattrocento: the medallions by Giotto and Pisano, the 'Cantoria' by Donatello and that of Luca della Robbia, the sixteen admirable statues that decorated the niches of the Campanile (by Pisano, Donatello, Nanni di Bartolo), and the celebrated 'Zuccone'.*

The Renaissance witnessed extreme and contradictory passions – tyranny, violence, cupidity, compassion, humility, holiness – which, if one excepts the purifying struggle led by Savonarola, existed side by side rather than in conflict one with the other. Stendhal saw this as a beneficial climate for art; he thought that it was the energy of the passions, both vices and virtues, that engendered masterpieces and that, when the storm has subsided, 'everything becomes small, insignificant and distorted'. Amid the cynical tyrannies of the thirteenth and fourteenth centuries, when lords and soldiers of fortune (*condottieri*) swept away the old liberties, the privileged economic and social situation enjoyed by both Venice and Florence was to stimulate a sudden cultural flowering.

Elsewhere, good and evil were found mixed in surprising proportions: the cruelty of the Visconti in Milan was counterbalanced by the enlightened authority exercised by the dukes of Mantua, Ferrara and Urbino. But it was in Florence and in Tuscany as a whole that the blossoming of Man, the confidence in his almost limitless possibilities and the ideal of beauty and harmony, were most powerfully asserted. As Jacob Burckhardt, the great historian of the Renaissance, has written, 'Florence was engaged in the broadest development of individualities at a time when the tyrants admitted no individuality other than their own.'

p. 34

left DETAIL OF THE PIETÀ *(1555), one of the last of Michelangelo's sculptures and one of his most powerfully dramatic works. Michelangelo is supposed to have intended this statue for his own tomb and to have represented himself, in the guise of Joseph of Arimathea, dressed in his simple woollen robe (Duomo).*

right DETAIL OF THE CANTORIA, *a marble choir-loft carved (1431–1438) for the cathedral by* LUCA DELLA ROBBIA. *It is supremely graceful and yet possesses a strikingly natural quality (Museo dell' Opera del Duomo).*

p. 35

THE CONDOTTIERE NICCOLÒ DA TOLENTINO *by* ANDREA DEL CASTAGNO *(1423–1457), a fresco which makes a pair with that of Paolo Uccello. Andrea del Castagno, one of the most personal and vigorous painters of the Quattrocento, is said also to have been on occasions a hired assassin.*
The 'condottieri' were the scourge of the fourteenth century; they commanded the mercenaries engaged in the numerous civil wars of the peninsula, wars which were not particularly bloody, but in which everyone tried to enrich himself and to extend his property. Nearly always cruel rogues, the 'condottieri' were feared even by their employers, who often held their wives and children as pledges of their loyalty.

2

SANTA CROCE – PAZZI CHAPEL – BARGELLO MUSEUM – FIESOLE.

Once the visitor has passed through the unprepossessing nineteenth-century façade of Santa Croce, the great Franciscan church of Florence, he will probably be surprised by the grace, sobriety and spaciousness of its nave. It was designed to accommodate large crowds, as can be seen by its imposing dimensions (one hundred and fifteen metres long, forty metres wide).

The Dominicans and Franciscans, the two mendicant orders, played an important part in the life of the Italian cities in the thirteenth and fourteenth centuries. Dominic, born in Castile in 1170, and Francis, born at Assisi in 1182,

were contemporaries and, though quite different in character, they were both to rekindle religious sentiment. St Francis visited Florence in 1211 and this avaricious city gave the 'Poverello' an enthusiastic welcome. The Franciscans devoted their attentions chiefly to the poor people of the suburbs and it was on the site of a chapel dedicated to Santa Croce (Holy Cross), outside the walls of the city, that construction of the present church began in the middle of the thirteenth century (work on the building was to continue for more than a hundred years). It seems that the extent to which St Francis's simplicity and love of Nature influenced the artists of his time has often been exaggerated. Although the *Hymn to the Sun* and the *Sermon to the Little Birds* might appear to contain a 'naturalist' message, the son of the wealthy cloth-merchant of Assisi did not himself encourage religious art; in fact, it was his wish that the place of worship should itself take a vow of poverty. But, a few decades after his death, his precepts had been forgotten and the originally modest basilica at Assisi, built to house his tomb, had a more elegant Gothic church built on to it and the whole was covered with frescoes. These frescoes were to play a determining role in the development of Tuscan art. It was here that Cimabue gave a new, Western inflexion to Byzantine traditions and that Giotto, commissioned in 1296 to retrace the life of St Francis, was able to transfer to painting the conquests which Gothic art had already made in stone.

Santa Croce is undoubtedly the church dearest to the hearts of the Florentines. Perhaps this is partly because it symbolizes the simplicity characteristic of the city's churches, a simplicity which is not to be found at Siena, Rome or Venice, and which gives them an austere grace and a true spirituality. But, above all, it is because Santa Croce contains the tombs of the most famous citizens of the City of the Arts: Ghiberti, Michelangelo, Machiavelli and Galileo. One would have wished to find their names commemorated on simple tombstones like those in the paving of the floor. The enterprising Vasari, however, had other ideas and placed cold, heavy tombs and altars along the walls of the side-aisle. Yet the atmosphere is none the less moving; it is known how devoted the Renaissance cities were to the remains of great men. Ravenna always refused to surrender the body of Dante and at Santa Croce the illustrious exile is commemorated only by a cenotaph.

The Pazzi Chapel, situated between the church and the main cloister, is a jewel of elegance and one of the most original works of Filippo Brunelleschi (1377–1446). Brunelleschi is certainly the most important artist in the history of Florence, and the city owes its finest monuments to him: the cupola of the Cathedral, the Hospital of the Innocents, the chapel of the Old Sacristy of San Lorenzo, and Santo Spirito. His conceptions were so novel and so convincing that even Michelangelo could only repeat them.

At first a goldsmith and sculptor, Brunelleschi only became an architect as he approached the age of forty, but from then onwards he worked tirelessly and his activity was to have a determining influence on the course of Western architecture. He spent a long period in Rome with Donatello, after their failure in the competition for the doors of the Baptistry in 1402. Despite his archaeological studies, he was probably influenced more by the Early Christian art of the fifth and sixth centuries and the Romanesque art of the eleventh and twelfth centuries than by Antiquity itself; like all Florentines, he was a descendant of the Etruscans and he seemed instinctively to rediscover their heritage, while his Latin sensibility remained foreign to Gothic art. In the work of Brunelleschi everything is subjected to a clear and rigorous order. André Chastel, a perceptive art historian, remarks that 'the volumes are treated as an articulation of surfaces, the surfaces as a function of the main lines, whose tension creates a natural beauty'.

The first of a new race of artists fascinated by the sciences, Brunelleschi discovered how to reduce a building to mathematical rules: in drawing up his plans he used the works of the great mathematician Toscanelli, his teacher and friend. He created abstract forms in stone which seemed the ideal of wisdom; it has even been said that a window designed by Brunelleschi represented the very concept of a window.

In his personal life Brunelleschi was a man of great simplicity. He was much loved by his fellow citizens, and his modesty and good humour were the subject of countless anecdotes. He was the creator of a supreme architecture and his work expresses the rarest virtues of Florence: simplicity, elegance, fullness, and the austere grace which is peculiar to the city.

THE PAZZI CHAPEL *was built for the illustrious family who were the rivals of the Medici. The plan of this graceful and beautifully balanced edifice is said to have been suggested to Brunelleschi by an Etruscan tomb. The portico is decorated with a delicate frieze designed by Donatello and carved by Desiderio da Settignano.*

THE CUPOLA *of the Pazzi Chapel epitomizes order and serenity. The grey stone of Florence, the 'pietra serena', emphasizes the lines and the disposition of space. The terracotta medallions of the Apostles and the Four Evangelists which adorn the vaults and the cupola are by* LUCA DELLA ROBBIA.

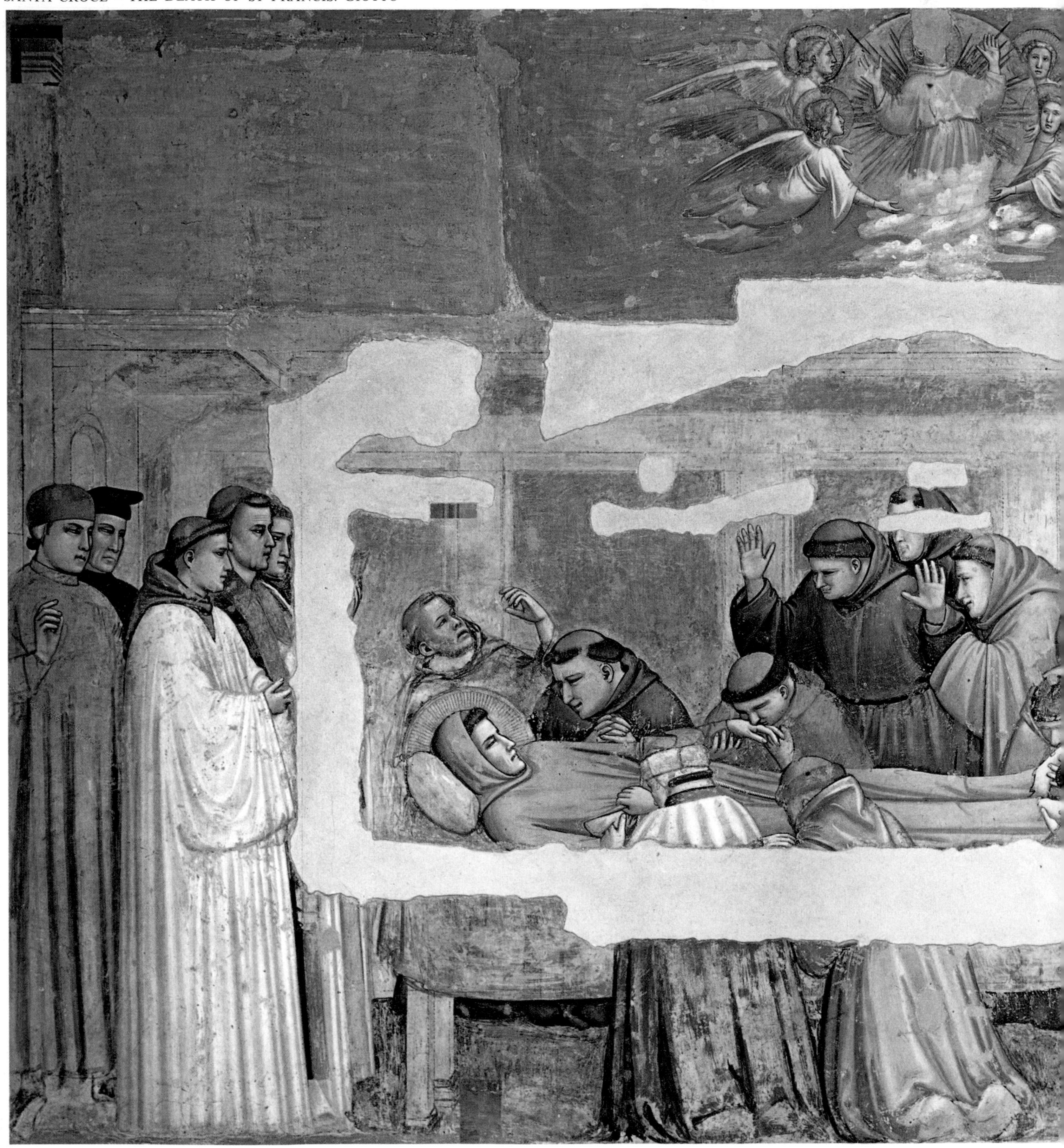

Giotto (1266–1337) was the first of the great Florentine painters. His most significant achievement is the series of frescoes in the Scrovegni Chapel at Padua (1303–1305), but the much later paintings in the two chapels of Santa Croce also bear witness to his genius. *St Francis on his deathbed surrounded by his friars* (1320) is an outstanding painting.

The art of Giotto reveals one of the most powerful creative forces that painting has ever known. All is design and architecture, and every line is essential. The figures are bulky and stiff, but they are alive and they move. As if under a spell, we believe in this reality which is not truly reality. Giotto sought to represent as intensely and as faithfully as possible, and this vision of the external comes from within, from the artlessness, the faith and the genius of the artist. Even if his painting is for many people merely a transcription of the expressionism of Gothic statuary, even if it is not completely free of Byzantine traditions and lacks the virtuosity of certain Hellenistic frescoes, it reveals something quite new: the subordination of the figures to a higher order which arranges and dominates them.

The son of a peasant of Colle di Vespignano, a village near Florence, Giotto, so serious in his art, was according to the chronicler 'an ugly, squat little man with a pug jaw, full of joy, lively, gay, waggish, rich in witticisms, a typically Florentine lover of jokes, tireless in his work, as simple and fertile as corn'.

In its universality the poetic imagination of Giotto recalls that of Dante. There is sublimity in his art, and in this rare quality only Rembrandt and Goya are his equals.

The roofs of Florence are infinite in their variety and yet blend in delightful harmony. Here the city is seen from the upper floor of Orsanmichele. In the distance stands San Miniato; on the left the graceful outlines of the Bargello Tower and the campanile of the Church of the Badia, an old Benedictine monastery founded in the tenth century and subsequently reconstructed.

In the eleventh and early twelfth centuries, towers stood everywhere round the present Piazza della Signoria and the old market. There were over a hundred, the powerful and insolent emblems of feudalism. In 1250, the year of the first Florentine democracy, the *primo popolo* ordered that the height of the towers be reduced by two-thirds.

Today, with the domes and bell-towers of the great churches, only the two Gothic towers still rise above the city: the Palazzo Vecchio and the Bargello Tower, the symbols of the authority of the Commune. The Palazzo del Podestà, or Bargello, is a remarkable example of a thirteenth-century fortified palace. The disposition of its courtyard, lined with arches, reveals a more attractive Gothic style of the fourteenth century. Fixed on the walls in noble disorder are the coats of arms of the *podestà* (the chief magistrates) and those of the different quarters of the city, carved in stone. This is one of the places in Florence where the presence of history is most vividly felt.

The Bargello was begun in 1254 to serve as a residence for the 'captain of the people', the highest office established by the first democratic government inaugurated four years earlier. So that they might be less concerned with local interests and passions, both the 'captain of the people' and, later, the *podestà* had to be strangers to the city. The *primo popolo* also decided that the lily, the city's emblem, would no longer be white but red, and chose the lion as the symbol of the people's government. According to Dante, the ten blessed years of the *primo popolo* were the only years of civil peace that Florence enjoyed in the Middle Ages.

In the Quattrocento, as in the preceding centuries, sculpture was the supreme art, at first because of its social

Two masterpieces by DONATELLO *(1386–1466). At the back, in its stone niche, is the statue of* ST GEORGE, *patron saint of the armourers' guild, which originally stood in Orsanmichele, where it is now replaced by a bronze copy. In the foreground, the famous* DAVID *(1430). The graceful workmanship of this bronze is quite different from that of the more sober 'St George' of twenty-five years earlier. The Renaissance had finally found its style. This statue, commissioned by Cosimo the Elder, was probably the first nude since Antiquity.*

p. 45
ST JOHN BAPTIST. *If, as is believed, this marble was carved by Donatello, it reveals yet another aspect of his talent. Here realism is mingled with tenderness and spirituality. Donatello's concern with truth was to drive him even further, to the utter pathos of the wonderful 'St Mary Magdalene' in the Baptistry which he carved during the last years of his life. The thirst for realism that inspired the artists of the early Quattrocento is vividly expressed by Donatello's supposed cry to his famous statue of the 'Zuccone': 'Favelle! Favelle!' ('Speak! Speak!').*

function, which was to adorn religious and civic buildings, to give expression to feelings of veneration or esteem, or simply to satisfy the inhabitants' taste for beauty; and later, because its very form seemed the most noble. Sculpture is an art that suppresses all superfluous matter and retains only the essential, whereas painting, by contrast, emerges from successive additions. The Neo-Platonic humanism of the Renaissance discovered in sculpture the very principle of Socratic thought: gradually to remove the superfluous in order to arrive at the essential.

Donatello is the master of all sculptors. Michelangelo is an artist apart, less a Florentine than passionately himself. Donatello *is* Florence, 'happy and rich Florence which triumphs in politics and in the arts, still republican and yet subject to the prince, thoroughly Christian in its manners and yet a little pagan in spirit'. In his long life of eighty-five years, Donato di Bardi, known as 'Donatello', the son of a wool-carder, also embodied the whole fifteenth century.

Looking at the stone *St George* (1416), destined to adorn a niche in Orsanmichele, and then the bronze *David* commissioned by Cosimo the Elder (1430), one senses the excitement of the period. Artists were embarking on a thrilling adventure: they were discovering Man and the world. Donatello was influenced by ancient models to a much greater degree than Brunelleschi, his friend and his companion on the journey to Rome. While the *St George*, superb in its strength, still possesses a Gothic balance, the graceful, lissom body of the *David* is the Renaissance itself. There is here a vigour and elegance which constitute the genius of this artist. Yet, though perhaps more truly a sculptor than Giotto was a painter, Donatello is much less a poet; he touches and he charms, but he does not make one think. Possibly because he was endowed with facility no less than with genius, facility often overshadows genius in his works. His virtuosity, and also the vigour of which he was sometimes capable, appear in the great equestrian statue of the *condottiere* Gattamelata which he executed at Padua (1444–1447), taking his inspiration from the statue of Marcus Aurelius that he had seen in Rome. His *David* is believed to have been the first nude of the Renaissance; his *Gattamelata* was its first giant statue.

It was Donatello in sculpture who, like Masaccio in painting, broke finally with the medieval and Gothic tradition. After assimilating in dazzling fashion the lessons of Antiquity, without ever becoming its slave, he found a new form of art that would satisfy the ideal of beauty of his time.

At the beginning of the celebrated Quattrocento, artists, both sculptors and painters, were still regarded simply as craftsmen. They were poorly paid and depended

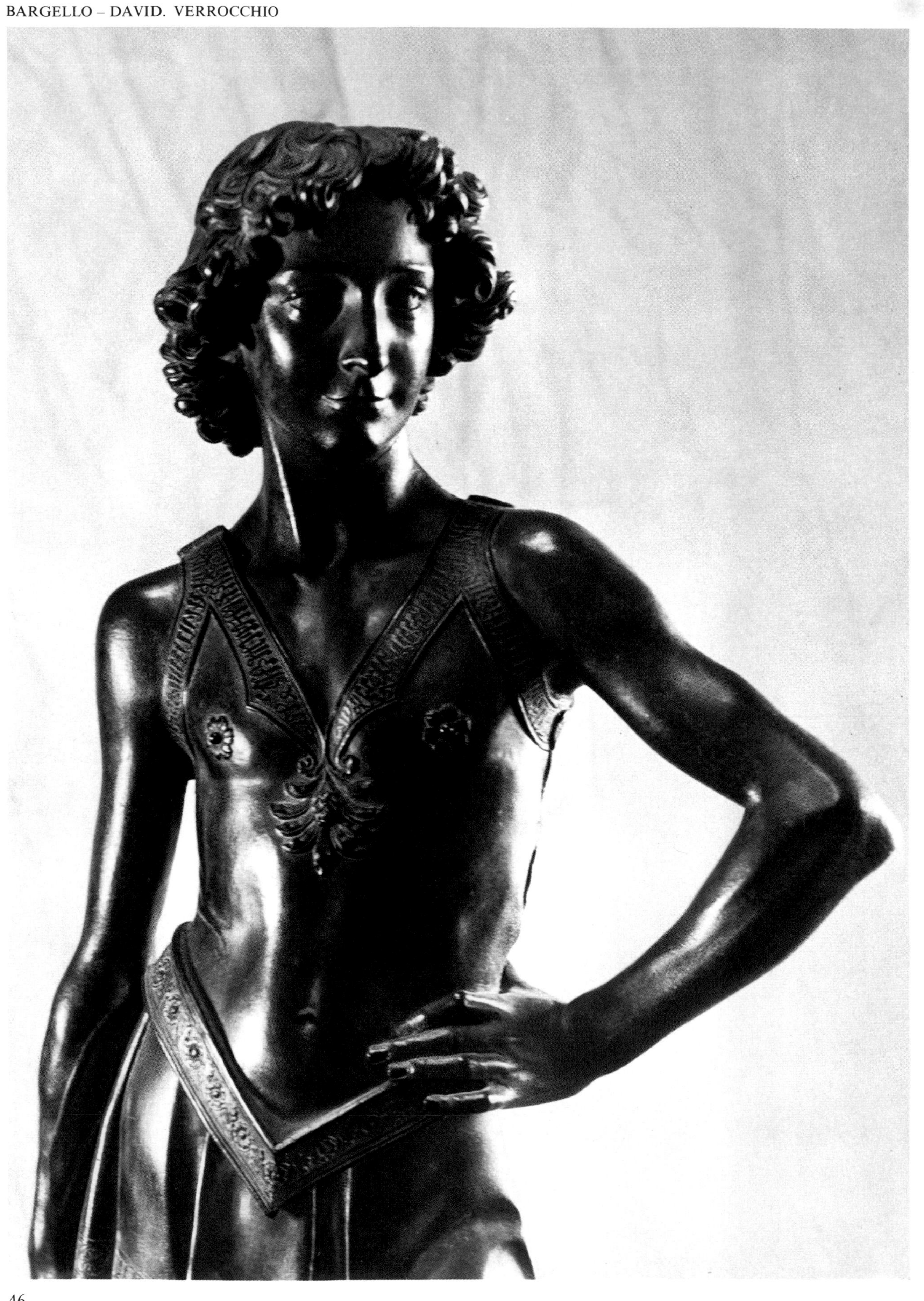

DAVID, *a bronze by Verrocchio (1435–1488), more virile and radiant than that of his master Donatello. It is the essence of the Renaissance, the expression of joy and youth.*

p. 47
THE GRAND COUNCIL CHAMBER, *which houses the masterpieces from the golden age of Renaissance statuary (the first half of the Quattrocento).*

on the commissions of the clergy, the guilds and a few wealthy families. All had issued from the lower orders of society, the sons of peasants and workmen. Some had at first been simple stone-cutters in the quarries of Carrara; most of them had worked with the master-goldsmiths, from whom they received their training. The development of commerce and the wealth of the great banks were to give the arts of the fifteenth century a role and a brilliance without precedent. The Florentines, who had always had a keen municipal awareness, took a passionate interest in the new buildings and embellishments of their city, encouraging or finding fault with the artists responsible. Donatello used to say in jest that he would soon have to leave Padua, where he was showered with praise but where he was achieving nothing worthwhile, for Florence where, constantly criticized, he found stimulation and made progress. Yet, in spite of the interest which they attracted, architects and sculptors lived in hardship. Donatello had a reputation for never refusing a commission, however modest, and the story goes that he was

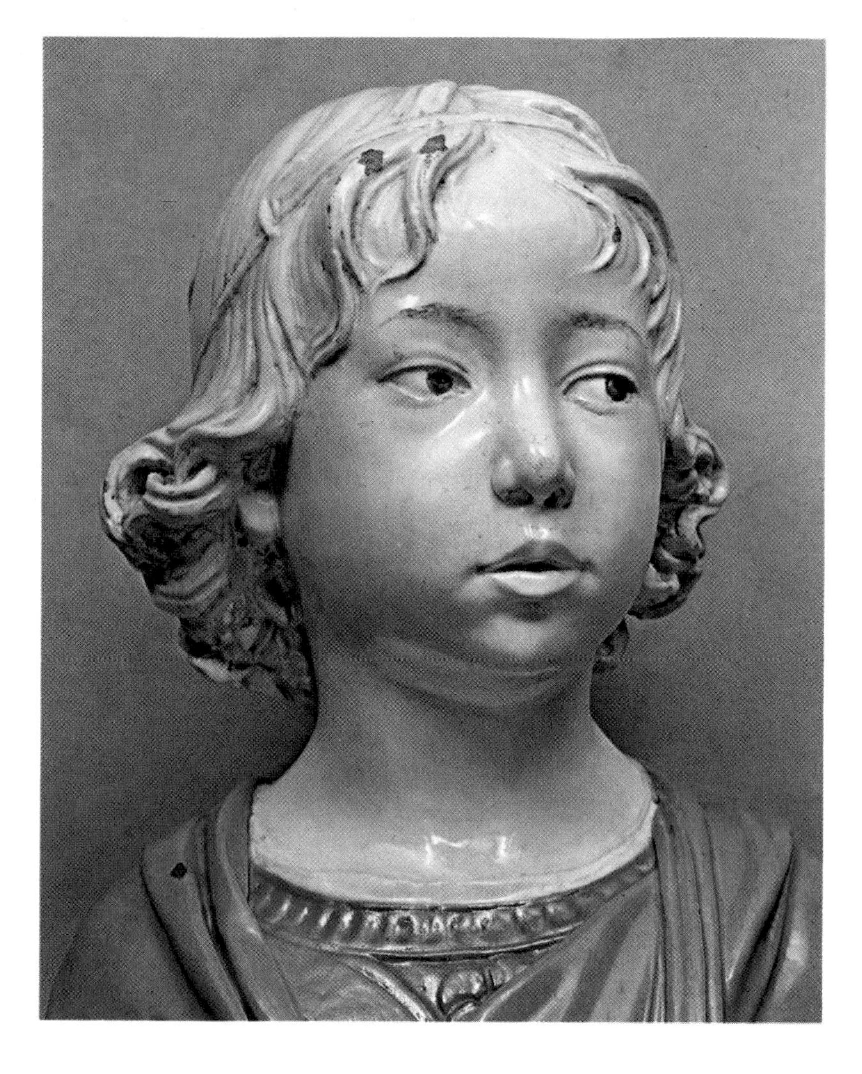

BUSTS OF A WOMAN AND A CHILD. *Glazed polychrome terracottas by* LUCA DELLA ROBBIA *(1400–1482).*
This technique of 'glazed' sculpture, original and delicate, rapidly became popular and was cultivated as a decorative element, often in the form of medallions or 'tondi' framed by garlands of flowers.
The workshop of Luca della Robbia consequently became extremely active and the artist passed on the secrets of his technique to his nephew Andrea. Andrea's sons, Giovanni, Girolamo and Luca, carried on the family tradition in the early sixteenth century, but the technique disappeared with them.

p. 48
BUST OF NICCOLÒ DA UZZANO, *a painted terracotta attributed to* DONATELLO *(1386–1466).*
This is without doubt one of the first portraits of the Renaissance. Niccolò da Uzzano lived at the time when the Medici and the Albizzi were struggling for power; during these years of petty intrigues and rivalries, he proved to be one of the wisest and staunchest citizens of Florence.

Amid the tumults and rivalries of the Quattrocento, nobility of character still existed; these faces could almost belong to patricians of the glorious epoch of the Roman Republic. It was the ambition of Florence's most noble citizens, faithful to the teaching of their great idol, Cicero, to be the pillars of the political life and of the virtue of their city.

obliged to borrow a doublet for his presentation to Cosimo the Elder.

It seems that a real fellow-feeling existed among these artists; they lived together and their lives were sober, hard and virile. The majority remained unmarried and special affections often developed between masters and apprentices. They worked together on the big building-sites, but it was not until the second half of the fifteenth century that large workshops, like those of della Robbia, Verrocchio and Ghirlandaio, were established to meet an increasing demand.

Brunelleschi and Donatello heralded the springtime of the Renaissance. Although they exchanged ideas and advice, and although they worked together in close partnership on the Sacristy of San Lorenzo, each of them lived his own personal adventure none the less intensely; they sought glory, but they had no material ambitions. By the end of the fifteenth century it was quite a different matter: the greatest artists, sought after by the cities of Italy and by the neighbouring kingdoms, and invited to the tables of popes and kings, became used to fame and affluence.

The artists of the beginning of the Quattrocento lived through the most exalting years of the Renaissance. They were awakening to a new world. They discovered the free and sensual forms of Antiquity and cast off the fetters of the religious subject. This was the end of Scholasticism and its clearly defined compartments, and the beginning of a living culture. These men took an interest in everything: Brunelleschi was draughtsman, architect, sculptor and engineer; Donatello was a collector of antiques and Ghiberti a writer. For them the boundary between science and art no longer existed. Later, this universality was to be pushed to its limits by the genius of Leonardo da Vinci. In the history of art, the beginning of the Quattrocento is one of those periods when an ideal balance seems to have been established between the natural, instinctive forces in man and the forces of knowledge, leading to the creation of the most noble and sincere works of art. These artists had preserved their simplicity intact. A peasant vigour and a craftsman's modesty nurtured works of brilliance and vitality. The blossoming of these men was a natural process; ideas uplifted them, but did not dominate them. In their art there was the joy of

THE MARBLE BUST OF PIETRO MELLINI *by* BENEDETTO DA MAIANO *(1442–1497) is full of life and delicacy.*
The works of Benedetto da Maiano, sculptor and architect, are to be found in abundance in Florence: the carved ceilings of the Palazzo Vecchio, the magnificent Palazzo Strozzi and the marble pulpit in Santa Croce carved with scenes from the life of St Francis.

BUST OF A GIRL. *Marble carved by* DESIDERIO DA SETTIGNANO *(1428–1464), of a thoroughly Florentine sensitivity and delicacy.*

p. 51
MARBLE BUST OF A YOUNG WOMAN. *The work of* ANDREA VERROCCHIO *(1435–1488), striking in its intensity and refinement.*
A pupil of Donatello, goldsmith, sculptor, painter and a great draughtsman, Verrocchio was the teacher of Perugino and Leonardo da Vinci. The attribution of certain works sometimes leads to confusion between Verrocchio and his most famous pupil, Leonardo. Verrocchio was interested in the exact sciences and, like Leonardo, recognized the close links between beauty and knowledge.

discovery, but as yet no conscious intention. The Renaissance had the freshness and beauty of adolescence.

After visiting the masterpieces of the great Florentine sculptors, you can go in search of the fresh air and natural surroundings to which they owed part of their genius, in the countryside around Florence.

It would be difficult to imagine more delicate and graceful countryside than the hill of Fiesole, a few kilometres from Florence. Cypresses, vines and olive trees cover the gentle slopes which run down towards the city and the contrasts of their greens give a strength to the subtle blend of colours. Fiesole, the mother of Florence and once an Etruscan and Roman city, is a delightful place with its peaceful monastery of San Francesco and its Roman theatre. On the slopes of the hill stand the Villa Palmieri, in the gardens of which Boccaccio is said to have set *The Decameron*, and a Medici villa, a simple country-house built by Michelozzo for Cosimo the Elder.

p. 52

THE MONASTERY OF SAN FRANCESCO *looks over the valley of the Arno; built by the Dominicans in the thirteenth century, it was subsequently occupied by the Franciscans.*

THE ROMAN THEATRE *dates from the time of Sulla (first century B.C.); it was transformed by the emperors Claudius and Septimius Severus. The stage has as its backcloth the beautiful hills of the Mugello.*

p. 53

VIEW OF FIESOLE. *Fiesole was a flourishing Etruscan city at the time when Rome was only a village. It was savagely destroyed by its rival, Florence, in 1125.*

THE VILLA MEDICI. *In this rustic villa Lorenzo de' Medici received his humanist friends Marsilio Ficino, Poliziano and Pico della Mirandola, and also numerous artists, physicians and merchants who shared his passion for Antiquity.*

THE BADIA FIESOLANA. *This church, situated on the hillside, has the simple charm of a hermitage. From here the view of Florence is wonderful. When Brunelleschi rebuilt the church at the request of Cosimo the Elder, he preserved the old façade, of a pure Romanesque style (eleventh century).*

Five centuries separate the façade of the Badia and the Italian-style gardens of the VILLA GAMBERAIA, *and yet in their geometric balance and their graceful, slightly austere disposition, they are not really so different.*
The Gamberaia looks out over Settignano which, despite the ravages of war, has retained its charm; in this village, as in its neighbours Fiesole and Maiano, many Renaissance artists were born, among them Mino, Rossellino, Desiderio, Bernardino and Fra Angelico.

From Fiesole to Settignano, and then from Settignano to the two Medici villas of Castello and Petraia, little roads run over the hills and among the cypresses and olive trees.

THE VILLA OF CASTELLO, *refashioned in the eighteenth century, was badly damaged during the war. Though much changed, the garden laid out by Tribolo, the great landscape-architect of Cosimo I, twenty years before he began work on the Boboli Gardens, is still one of the first examples of the 'Italian gardens' which became fashionable in the sixteenth century, with its geometric design and its statues, grottoes and fountains. The villa, which is in the process of being restored, is eventually to become a museum of frescoes, which are being removed from many buildings in Florence so that they can be preserved.*

THE VILLA OF PETRAIA, *rebuilt in the sixteenth century by Buontalenti, is a handsome edifice. In deciding on the layout of the garden Ferdinando de' Medici, first a cardinal and then grand duke in 1587, was influenced by the Villa d'Este at Tivoli, built thirty years earlier by the Cardinal d'Este. On the highest terrace a fountain-basin by Tribolo is surmounted by a graceful statue by Giambologna,* VENUS RISING FROM THE WATER. *Born at Douai in 1529, Giambologna was one of the most captivating artists of the closing sixteenth century, when Florentine art was entering its decline.*

3

SANTA MARIA DEL CARMINE – SANTO SPIRITO – OLTRARNO – UFFIZI GALLERY.

More than a century separated Giotto and Masaccio and during this time Florentine painting had shown no essential character of its own. Then suddenly, when the delicate Gothic style of Lorenzo Monaco and Gentile da Fabriano was at the height of its success, there appeared an art of astounding maturity and expressive power.

Masaccio played in painting a role no less revolutionary than Brunelleschi in architecture and Donatello in sculpture, and in fact his art owed much to Donatello. Some ten square yards of frescoes in the Brancacci Chapel of the Church of Santa Maria del Carmine show the beginning not only of Renaissance painting, but of Western painting for centuries to come. These frescoes reveal totally new conquests: an adroit and exact use of perspective with the figures modelled to stand out in their true dimensions. If one compares Masaccio's frescoes with the paintings of his great Flemish contemporaries, van Eyck and van der Weyden, one discovers that in the works of those two artists landscapes and figures are still bound by conventions, whereas in Masaccio they are the expression of a reality; under his brush naturalism, the most solid achievement of Renaissance painting, was born. In his composition there is a calm and a grandeur which only the greatest artists of the

seventeenth century, Velázquez and Poussin, were able to emulate.

Masaccio is not, perhaps, as much a poet as Giotto, but no one was more a painter. Giotto's human figures are the elements of the mystery that dominates them; those of Masaccio exist for themselves, they belong wholly to this epoch when Man was discovering himself and beginning to believe in himself. One can understand Bernard Berenson's admiration of Masaccio's frescoes: 'Then what strength to his young men, and what gravity and power to his old!'

Masaccio died in Rome at the age of twenty-seven. His work, although spanning so brief a time, had far-reaching influence: the Renaissance artists immediately recognized their master and even the greatest went to the chapel of Santa Maria del Carmine to learn from him.

The church of Santa Maria del Carmine, founded at the same time as a friary by the hermits of the Penitent Order of Mount Carmel which had come to Italy from the Holy Land in the thirteenth century, was almost completely destroyed by a fire in 1771. It is a miracle that the Brancacci Chapel, whose frescoes are one of the essential elements of the history of Florentine painting, was spared.

The vast Piazza del Carmine lies at the heart of the working-class quarter of the Oltrarno, known as the 'Borgo San Frediano'. It was a peaceful, rustic place before, like all the squares in Florence, it was invaded by cars.

What the Trastevere is to Rome, the Oltrarno is to Florence. It is here that the real heart of the city beats. This is where the ordinary people are to be found, warm-hearted, excitable and with their mischievous sense of humour, and where the past remains most alive. The Via Sant'Agostino cuts across the Via Serragli, lined with numerous palaces interspersed with the shops of craftsmen and antique-dealers, and leads into the Piazza Santo Spirito, a popular and colourful spot. Behind the market which is often held on the square, the simple and original façade of Santo Spirito is one of the classic sights of Florence. Its design does not correspond exactly with the plans prepared by Brunelleschi two years before his death. The interior, with its measured harmony of white and grey, is more faithful to the great architect. The colonnade which runs along the two side-aisles, comprising thirty-five Corinthian columns, is breathtaking in its lightness and grace. The octagonal chapel and its vestibule, the work of Giuliano da Sangallo, are also faithful to the spirit of Brunelleschi. Numerous works by Filippo Lippi, Lorenzo di Credi, Bernardo Daddi, Ghirlandaio, Bernardo Rossellino and Neri di Bicci decorate the thirty-eight chapels.

Wandering through the Oltrarno, one realizes that its squares and churches are enclosed like suns in a dark network of delightful narrow streets where, as Stendhal wrote, one still finds the imprint of medieval passions. One of the pleasures of Florence is to stroll through these old districts and discover the noble, emblazoned portals of the palaces and their sumptuous courtyards which the visitor comes across so unexpectedly. The Via Maggio, which is a continuation of Via Tornabuoni on the other side of the Arno, is the most popular and majestic of these streets; in earlier days the processions and masquerades came this way. Near the Palazzo Pitti, it is lined with mansions that belonged to the members of the grand-ducal court: the Casa Corsini, the Palazzo Biliotti, and the Palazzo Cappello which Buontalenti refashioned in 1570 for the beautiful Venetian Bianca Cappello, who became the mistress and then the wife of Grand Duke Francesco I. The couple were to die together in mysterious circumstances at the villa of Poggio a Caiano, in 1587; rather than a romantic death-pact in the style of Mayerling, this was probably a case of poisoning and the work of the grand duke's brother, Cardinal Ferdinando, who as Ferdinando I proved an energetic administrator.

The districts of Santo Spirito and San Frediano have always been occupied by the craftsmen of Florence, who still have many stalls and workshops here. Even today one can find forges similar to that in which Niccolò Grosso, the fifteenth-century master-blacksmith, made the beautiful standard-holders adorning the Palazzo Strozzi. Sometimes, at the corner of a street, one finds a Baroque fountain or a tabernacle inviting the passer-by to pray.

Two symmetrical buildings, resting on two long colonnades and facing each other, extend from the Arno to the Piazza della Signoria. The Uffizi (Offices) were built by Vasari, at the command of Cosimo I, to house the offices of the administration of the grand duchy, which at this time occupied almost the whole of Tuscany. The private passage which ran along the upper storey of the Ponte Vecchio and linked the Palazzo Pitti and the Palazzo Vecchio, the seat of the government, was used every day by the grand duke and his friends. To make the walk more agreeable, the Medici had paintings and other works of art from their collections placed in the corridor that passed through the Uffizi; thus the first 'art gallery' was born.

Today the Uffizi is one of the most famous art galleries in the world and possesses one of the richest collections of masterpieces. Italian painting in general, and Tuscan painting in particular, are represented in magnificent style; Flemish and German artists are also represented by major works, recalling the commercial and financial relations which Florence maintained with Flanders and the political suzerainty exercised for centuries by Germany.

Antiquity did not directly influence the dawn of Italian painting, its frescoes and mosaics being at that time almost completely unknown. In fact, the origins of Italian painting date from the great migration of Byzantine artists in the eighth and ninth centuries. Monks from Greece, Egypt and Syria, victims of the iconoclast fury of the Emperors of the East that was to result in the disruption of the Christian world, came to seek refuge in Rome. Even if this branch of Byzantine art was less vigorous and less original than that responsible for the admirable mosaics made in Rome and Ravenna in the fifth and sixth centuries, it influenced the Roman and Tuscan artists who decorated the basilica at Padua and who were the true originators of modern painting: first Cimabue, then Giotto and Duccio, the one devoting himself to forms and to composition, the other to the search for chromatic richness.

There followed a century of Gothic elegance in the course of which Simone Martini, Gentile da Fabriano and Lorenzo Monaco offered those shimmering, golden images of a divine world, and then there suddenly appeared the powerful art of Masaccio, leading the procession of the great painters who are the glory of Florence.

In the fourteenth and even at the beginning of the fifteenth century, the art of painting was not placed on the same level as architecture and sculpture. The Quattrocento was to give painting its letters of nobility. The Renaissance, when individuality asserted itself, was to witness the triumph of the art that allowed the most sensitive and personal expression. Yet one must not forget that the artists of Florence enjoyed a rare privilege – universality. Their curiosity and their abilities extended to all domains:

CIMABUE

sculpture, architecture, poetry, science. For many of them painting was the expression of only a part of their interests and their talents. Their thirst for knowledge was immense and they refused to be fettered by specialization; it was to this 'humanist' richness that they owed the intensity and profundity that was to characterize their art.

Later, Leonardo da Vinci was to embody the extreme achievement of this eclecticism. For this universal genius, art was merely a branch of knowledge. This mind of prodigious power in analysis and observation found in painting a means by which to attain a synthesis of his own knowledge, a synthesis into which he also put his feelings and which, for him, must have been a kind of relaxation. In his drawing and his painting he gave a form to the living, mysterious forces of Man, the interior light that illumines Man; and yet, if he rarely completed these works, it was doubtless because he considered them inferior to what he felt within himself, because he could not make himself master of everything that he wanted to bring into his art.

The first generation of painters of the Quattrocento were seeking the mastery of their art. Three contemporaries of Masaccio were to develop the discoveries which he himself seemed to have made so naturally.

DETAIL FROM THE VIRGIN IN MAJESTY *by* CIMABUE *(1240–1302).*

DETAIL FROM THE VIRGIN IN MAJESTY *by* GIOTTO *(1266–1337).*

pp. 68–69
THE ANNUNCIATION *(1333) by* SIMONE MARTINI. *This Sienese painter, following the manner of Duccio, lacked Giotto's concern with the expression of forms and of movement. His painting was inspired solely by the ideal of beauty. In this respect, he is the most enchanting of all Gothic painters. His great reputation caused him to be summoned to the papal court at Avignon. Unfortunately, the frescoes which he painted there have been ruined.*

GIOTTO

This is the central part of Paolo Uccello's painting; the other two parts are in the National Gallery in London and the Louvre in Paris; the three pictures, in a single frame, once decorated the bedroom of Lorenzo the Magnificent. The great battles of the fifteenth century lasted three or four hours only, and even the most murderous resulted in few deaths. The 'condottieri' and their troops took no risks; protected by strong armour, they surrendered at the first opportunity. It was a cunning game of chess which Chinese generals also liked to play, a game in which the victims were always the peasants. These make-believe soldiers, concerned only with gaining riches for themselves, had nothing in common with the citizens' armies of the time of Dante. The battles in which the latter fought were desperate and bloody affairs; at Campaldino, 1,700 Ghibellines were killed.
A contemporary of Masaccio, Paolo Uccello (1397–1475), like Andrea del Castagno, belonged to the 'conquering' phase of the Quattrocento. He was fascinated by perspective and geometric motifs, and his extravagances seem to foreshadow certain characteristics of the Cubists and the Fauves. He painted red meadows, blue towns and green horses. In fact, still influenced by the Gothic habits whose naïve freshness is to be seen in his landscapes, Uccello sought, in his study of lines and structures, not only a new form of expression, but also to analyse the world.

Paolo Uccello (1397–1475) was fascinated by perspective and the analysis of structures. Andrea del Castagno (1423–1457), with his brutal lines and implacable style, seems to have been obsessed by volumes and plastic tension. Domenico Veneziano (1400–1461) is a rather mysterious artist; according to Vasari, the painters of the Quattrocento owed much to him. A Venetian by birth, Domenico arrived in Florence with a mastery of the technique of oils and the secret of light, clear colours. He initiated a style of painting in which the colouring is unified in a diffused light; the fluidity of space that one finds in his pictures gives the architecture and the countryside a new value. Domenico

also had a keen appreciation of the human face and was probably the first to give his figures an individuality that was to lead to the portrait. Under his influence emerged the prince of Renaissance painters, Piero della Francesca (1410–1492). It was perhaps because he divided his life between the villages of his childhood, Arezzo and Borgo San Sepolcro, and the ducal courts of Ferrara and Urbino to which he was called, that this painter had such a strong feeling for Nature and, at the same time, a gift for the noble and solemn arrangement of human figures. Piero della Francesca has his own personal world, both calm and rigorous, virile and majestic. The impassive and impersonal quality of his faces arouses deeper sentiments than more expressive faces would; if there is in him less life and less strength than in Masaccio, there is a greater mystery. Like Baldovinetti, another pupil of Veneziano, he gave landscape a new importance, almost making it an end in itself. Behind the rustic or aristocratic dignity of the figures there appears, in a yellow light, the sharply defined contours of the hills of Umbria or of Tuscany. This magnificent artist was fascinated by the exact sciences; he wrote a treatise on perspective and an essay on pure matter, and devoted the last years of his life to the study of mathematics.

The artists born between 1430 and 1445 formed the

PORTRAITS OF FEDERICO DA MONTEFELTRO, DUKE OF URBINO, AND HIS WIFE BATTISTA SFORZA, *by* PIERO DELLA FRANCESCA *(1410–1492). Federicò da Montefeltro was an enlightened prince and an accomplished warrior whose services were sought by Lorenzo the Magnificent against Volterra. The duke of Urbino, who lost his right eye and had his nose broken in a tournament, is always portrayed in profile.*

p. 73
SPRING *(detail) by* SANDRO BOTTICELLI *(1445–1510). This picture, like the 'Birth of Venus', another famous work by Botticelli, seems to have been painted to glorify the 'Venus humanitas' dear to the Neo-Platonists of Lorenzo the Magnificent's circle, and which symbolized the idea of a higher culture embracing philosophy, poetry, art, science, love and pedagogy.*

THE ADORATION OF THE MAGI *(1481). Detail. An unfinished work of* LEONARDO DA VINCI *(1452–1519). After enjoying the patronage of Lorenzo the Magnificent, Leonardo left Florence at the age of thirty for Milan, where he was summoned by Ludovico the Moor, not as a painter but for his talents as a musician. Thereafter, he only returned for short visits to the city of his youth. The long and faithful patronage of the Sforza family was followed by that of Charles d'Amboise, Louis XII's governor of Milan, and then Giuliano de' Medici. On the death of this prince Leonardo accepted the generous invitation of Francis I, who admired him and wanted to be able to converse with him. During the three years that he spent in France, it seems, he abandoned artistic activity. He died at the château of Cloux at Amboise, on 2nd May 1519.*

p. 75

HERCULES AND ANTAEUS *by* ANTONIO DEL POLLAIUOLO *(1432–1498). The struggle between the Greek hero and the giant, the son of Poseidon, possesses a violence and a realism that are the mark of Antonio Pollaiuolo. According to the legend, Hercules, realizing that Antaeus was recovering his strength each time he touched the ground, held him up in his arms and thus succeeded in choking him.*

second generation of the Quattrocento. The heroic years were over, but artistic individuality remained a powerful force.

Botticelli (1445–1510) was one of the youngest of this generation and, although in the eyes of most people he symbolizes Florentine painting, he was an artist apart. He was a mystical person of great complexity. Once the joys of youth were past, he found himself torn apart by his contradictions: his sadness and his passion, his love of purity and of pleasure, his faith and his torments of doubt. The preaching of Savonarola affected him deeply in his old age. Botticelli heralds the crisis which marks the end of Medicean art, a crisis manifested by an exhaustion of ideas and most of all, after the boundless confidence of the earlier years, by doubts concerning the possibilities and destiny of Man.

The art of Botticelli, imbued with a captivating and, at the same time, almost irritating charm, is as mysterious as the artist. Everything – subject, composition, drawing, colours – is artificial; and yet this painting, dominated by outlines and arabesques, is as bewitching as a beautiful symphony. Behind its apparent indifference and the Neo-platonic intentions of its allegorical themes, it conceals the alluring and mysterious call of the unknown. At the time when everyone was paying homage to Leonardo, Botticelli remained faithful to his own linear system, with its feeble relief and uniform light. He spent the last years of his life illustrating the *Divine Comedy*.

Antonio del Pollaiuolo (1432–1498), goldsmith, maker of bronzes and a sculptor like his brother Piero, was considered the greatest artist of his time. Intrigued by the study of the human body and its muscular activity, he gave his paintings an extreme physical tension expressed by gestures and movements. He also had a sense of the harmony of space and a taste for landscape in the Flemish manner. In his works one feels a torment, a frantic desire to push his art to its limits; this tension gives his compositions an almost painful strength and originality.

Andrea Verrocchio (1435–1488), also at first a goldsmith and bronze-maker, then a great sculptor of movement with his masterpieces, the *Child with the Dolphin* at the Palazzo Vecchio and the equestrian statue of the *Colleoni* in Venice, was at the same time a draughtsman and painter of rare quality.

All the great artists of the Renaissance were admirable draughtsmen, but Verrocchio's drawing has an unusual grace and clarity. In his painting, landscape finds its individuality. For the first time effects of light convey a feeling of the freshness of dawn or the shadows of twilight. Even if, as the head of a workshop, Verrocchio often had to satisfy commercial demand, his work shows a precision and, at the same time, a certain abstruse quality

that reveals the man of science; in this respect, he probably had a powerful influence on his pupils Lorenzo di Credi and, in particular, Leonardo da Vinci.

Leonardo da Vinci (1452–1519), by his universality and his unique personality, does not really belong to the Florentine school. If the word 'genius' means anything at all, he was one of the greatest that humanity has known.

He analysed, understood and assimilated everything in art so that he might discover his own form of expression in which to interpret a personal universe. He was the most sensitive, exact and inventive of draughtsmen, with a sense of gesture and movement that has never been equalled. His paintings were for him the object of endless research and study, and yet they retain an intensity and mystery that faithfully reflect his inner radiance. The contrast of light and shade, and the delicacy of the 'velvet' texture, combine to encompass figures and landscape in a fabulous atmosphere that is neither gratuitous nor imaginary, but which expresses a sublimated vision of reality.

Florence has only one great painting by da Vinci, *The Adoration of the Magi* (1481), an unfinished work. One can only lament the disappearance of the huge fresco *The Battle of Anghiari* (1503–1505) which decorated the Grand

Council Chamber of the Palazzo Vecchio. To judge by the studies and the grisaille copy which Rubens made of a cartoon, it was a revolutionary painting: horses and riders had a prodigious quality of movement. In spite of the technical perfection of the composition and the drawing, there was in this fresco, as in *The Adoration of the Magi*, passion and turbulence. Leonardo da Vinci was foreshadowing Tintoretto, Rubens and Delacroix, and showing quite clearly that his art was foreign to the general trend of his epoch.

Two distinct paths can be traced in the painting of the Quattrocento. One, the path followed by Masaccio, Castagno, Pollaiuolo and Verrocchio, has the gravity and the colouring of autumn. It was here that the most important things happened, for this was the path of grandeur leading to the summits, Leonardo da Vinci and Michelangelo. The other path was full of joy and sun, with Filippo Lippi, Gozzoli, Ghirlandaio and Filippo's son, Filippino, walking amid the brilliant colours of spring. In the Victorian period these men were to bring the painting of the Quattrocento glory and popular renown, but, despite their charm and their skill, they were great artists only in their technique.

Fra Angelico (1387–1455) was the first to abandon the profound vision of Giotto, seeking instead to express his naïve faith in paintings of marvellous freshness and colour. The work of his pupil Benozzo Gozzoli (1420–1497) was that of a brilliant story-teller; he did not have the soul of his master and in his art he celebrated the glory of Man and not that of God. Filippo Lippi (1406–1469) also belonged to this line of great colourists; although possessing great skill, he too always remained on the dazzling surface of things.

Ghirlandaio (1449–1494) assimilated all the technical progress that had been made and, with his frescoes in Santa Trinità and Santa Maria Novella, proved himself a great decorative artist. He had an admirable descriptive sense, but he lacked personality and conviction; he holds the attention but, except in a few portraits, he never moves one. His highly receptive nature was captivated by the decorative composition and taste for detail revealed in the very beautiful and noble *Adoration of the Shepherds* by Hugo van der Goes. This Flemish painting arrived in Florence in 1481 and it was certainly not the first to have influenced the Italian artists. The landscapes and distant views of Piero della Francesca and Antonio Pollaiuolo must surely owe something to those of van Eyck.

Italy was undoubtedly in advance of the whole of Europe, but it did not create the Renaissance alone; it simply gave the most coherent, the newest and the richest expression to common aspirations which, in spite of the constraints of Gothic art, also existed in Flanders and in Burgundy.

The life of the inhabitants of Bruges, Brussels or Dijon in the fifteenth century was hardly different from that of the Florentines. The same enlightened patronage existed and the same problems preoccupied artists. The Flemish painters were advancing in their conquest of space and depth by feeling their way and by instinct, while the Florentines were pursuing the same goal rationally, using geometry and making perspective a science. The painters of the North, on the other hand, were the originators of the technique of oil.

THE VIRGIN AND CHILD WITH ST JOHN BAPTIST *by* FILIPPO LIPPI *(1406–1469). The manufacture of high-quality paper during the second half of the Quattrocento explains the new importance assumed by drawing and engraving. In addition to the traditional methods – the silver point, pen, brush and pencil (black stone) – red chalk and pastel were used towards the end of the century. Another refinement was the use of tinted paper (salmon-pink, grey and light blue). The highlights of white gouache reveal the ease and precision of expression acquired by artists such as Filippo Lippi and Lorenzo di Credi.*

p. 79
THE HOLY FAMILY *(1504) by* MICHELANGELO *(1475–1564). 'I am not a painter', Michelangelo would obstinately repeat to Pope Julius II, who became impatient at the slow progress of the decoration of the Sistine Chapel. In fact, only the painting of monumental frescoes suited the scale of his art. 'The Holy Family' is the only easel-painting that Michelangelo completed; he considered this art to be 'ladies' work'. Even in his paintings Michelangelo is primarily a sculptor. The cleanness of the contours gives the figures a striking relief. This youthful work reveals the artist's aspirations and the stylistic elements that were to inspire the Sistine frescoes: noble and vigorous figures, action contained within a small space, and the presence of the nude, the ideal interpretation of form. In this religious 'tondo' there is no apparent spirituality – only movement, form and beauty.*

Side by side with commercial exchanges, and in particular the wool and silver trades, artistic exchanges were taking place. Through the branches of their bank the Medici played an important part in these closer relations. It was Tommaso Portinari, their agent in Bruges, who in 1476 commissioned Hugo van der Goes to paint the triptych of *The Adoration of the Shepherds*; and, at a time when the civil portrait did not yet exist in Florence, Giovanni Arnolfini, another of their managers, commissioned Jan van Eyck to paint himself and his wife; the result was the masterpiece now in the National Gallery in London.

Michelangelo arrived on the scene like a hero of Antiquity; when doubt was invading the latter years of the Quattrocento, he affirmed the strength and the glory of Man. He was in advance of his century, but he was also its culmination. Donatello, Piero della Francesca and Pollaiuolo had already given form an expressive value, but Michelangelo made the nude his own and, in his Titan's hands, it became the most powerful interpretation of form.

The masterpiece of Michelangelo the painter is the ceiling of the Sistine Chapel. It is the form and the movement of the bodies that give the finest scenes – *The Creation* and *The Temptation* – their emotive power. But if one compares his *Adam and Eve driven out of Paradise* with the same scene painted by Masaccio in the Brancacci Chapel, one does not find the latter's intensity or its deep dramatic sense. Michelangelo is the personification of art for art's sake and of the rejection of the pleasures of feeling.

The painter's creative energies were monopolized by the decoration of the Sistine Chapel: the huge vault which occupied him for five years and then, much later, the wall of the *Last Judgement* where one senses the artist gradually being overcome by apathy. All the more reason to lament the loss of his finest painting, *The Battle of Cascina*, which adorned the Grand Council Chamber in the Palazzo Vecchio and which Michelangelo painted in rivalry with Leonardo da Vinci, who had undertaken *The Battle of Anghiari* a few months earlier. The subject chosen by Michelangelo ideally suited his art: a troop of soldiers taken unawares as they were bathing. The young Florentine artists, dazzled by the beauty of the bodies and captivated by the passionate quest for noble and expressive forms, bowed in homage. Not only did Michelangelo have a strong influence on his young contemporaries – Pontormo, Bronzino, Rosso and the entire Mannerist movement – but he was to become the god of Baroque art, the god of excess, providing justification for the exaggerations of his disciples.

THE HOLY FAMILY. MICHELANGELO

MOSES DEFENDING THE DAUGHTERS OF JETHRO *by* ROSSO FIORENTINO *(1494–1541). Rosso, a variable artist, but one who displayed a great boldness of composition and a highly original style, was called to France by Francis I in 1530. He designed and decorated the main gallery of the palace of Fontainebleau. He found a keen rival in Primaticcio, who was to obliterate a large part of his work at Fontainebleau.*

p. 81
Detail of the fresco of the ANNUNCIATION *by* PONTORMO *(1494–1557). Removed from the Church of Santa Felicità in 1967, this painting is among the Florentine frescoes which, after being displayed throughout Europe in a travelling exhibition, are to be assembled in a special museum.*

Vasari and Cellini jeered at the artistic eccentricities of Pontormo, Rosso and Bronzino, no doubt because all three were infinitely more original than themselves. A modern eye, however, can appreciate this Mannerist art. Admittedly, in the works of these painters fascinated by Michelangelo, the nude often becomes an obsession. But Pontormo was a great artist who painted some admirable decorative frescoes, notably the rustic scene in the lunette of the villa of Poggio a Caiano. Bronzino was a portraitist of striking vigour, while sometimes Rosso infused his compositions with a power which even the greatest Romantic artists never equalled.

4

SAN LORENZO – NEW SACRISTY – PALAZZO MEDICI-RICCARDI – ACADEMY OF FINE ARTS – PIAZZA SS. ANNUNZIATA – SAN MARCO – ORSANMICHELE.

The church of San Lorenzo, crowned by a majestic cupola, stands in an area of the city enlivened by the proximity of the central market. The severe brick façade remains unfinished; at the request of the Medici Pope Leo X, Michelangelo had prepared a design for a decoration and had made a model which can be seen in the Casa Buonarroti. Only the design for the interior wall of the church was executed. In front of the façade stands the statue of the *condottiere* Giovanni delle Bande Nere, the father of the first grand duke, Cosimo I; today the monument overlooks the mass of multi-coloured canvases that cover the market-stalls.

San Lorenzo was the parish church of the Medici and the name of the Roman deacon was often given to mem-

bers of the family. Here their children were baptized and married and their dead buried. The marriage of Lorenzo the Magnificent and Clarice Orsini was celebrated here with great splendour.

It was Giovanni di Bicci, founder of the Medici power and father of Cosimo the Elder, who, with a few wealthy friends, commissioned Brunelleschi to build a new church in 1423. San Lorenzo was the most ambitious undertaking of the great architect, who died in 1445 before completing it. The plan, in the form of a Latin cross with three aisles, is traditional; but Brunelleschi used Classical architectural elements, Corinthian columns and semicircular arches, to give the nave and the chancel a lightness enhanced by the sober grace of the blue-grey stone of Florence, the *pietra serena*, which stands out against the whiteness of the walls.

Donatello is buried in a chapel of San Lorenzo. The two bronze pulpits were among his last works and were completed by his pupils, Bellano and Bertoldo. The latter, who subsequently became curator of Lorenzo the Magnificent's collection of antiquities in the gardens of San Marco, is supposed to have given advice to the young Michelangelo. From these pulpits Savonarola preached some of his harshest diatribes, not hesitating to admonish the Medici family, the benefactors of the church.

The names of Brunelleschi and Donatello are associated in another Renaissance masterpiece, the Sagrestia Vecchia or Old Sacristy situated at the end of the left aisle. Here Brunelleschi applied the same conception of geometric harmony that he employed later in the Pazzi Chapel. Straight lines, rectangles, circles and triangles form a graceful framework surrounding the details of a refined decoration. Donatello executed a group of sculptures of great delicacy and sensitivity: the corner medallions, the four *tondi* of the lunettes, and the delicious frieze of cherubs' heads that runs round the Sacristy. He also carved the bronze doors of the two little sacristies and the bas-reliefs above them. The tomb of Giovanni di Bicci de' Medici and his wife Piccarda, under the marble table in the centre of the Sacristy, is also attributed to him, as is the delightful bust of the young St Lawrence, set on a low cupboard along the wall.

Finally, at the entrance to the Sacristy stands the tomb of Giovanni and Piero de' Medici, the sons of Cosimo the Elder; this noble sarcophagus, with its blend of bronze and porphyry, was the first important work of Verrocchio (1472) and was commissioned by Lorenzo the Magnificent in honour of his father, Piero the Gouty, and his uncle.

The New Sacristy, one of the most striking proofs of Michelangelo's genius, is symmetrical with the Old Sacristy; unfortunately there is no way in from the church and to reach the Medici chapels visitors must use

an outside entrance. Although a century separates the construction of the two buildings, Michelangelo remained faithful to Brunelleschi's architectural conception: Florentine refinement prevailed over the Roman taste for the grand style, and there is the same bareness and geometric sobriety. This severe and yet graceful edifice emphasizes the strength of the tombs; here the statue is no longer a decorative element, but the essential thing. Instead of competing with the architecture, it asserts itself, representing the triumph of the personal expression of the artist.

The construction of the New Sacristy, commissioned in 1521 to house the tombs of members of the Medici family by the natural son of Giuliano, Cardinal Giulio de' Medici (who some years later became Pope Clement VII), was to continue for twenty years, and even then it was never completed. Although two rather colourless persons, whose chief merit was that they died young, Giuliano, duke of Nemours, and Lorenzo, duke of Urbino, the son and grandson of Lorenzo the Magnificent, are immortalized in stone, the tomb of Lorenzo the Magnificent and his brother Giuliano, assassinated in the Pazzi conspiracy, was never begun. Ironically, these two proud men, whose sons became popes, rest in a simple grave near the wall where their tomb was to be built.

It has been observed with some justification that only the two seated figures – Lorenzo, the celebrated *pensieroso*, in his meditative attitude, and Giuliano, represented as the young military chief, the symbol of action – give a feeling of equilibrium. The four allegories, *Night, Day, Dusk* and *Dawn*, seem to be slipping from the narrow consoles on which Michelangelo placed them. These splendid female bodies have been called 'athletes with breasts' and the absence of expression in the faces has also been emphasized. Nevertheless, this group of sculptures is one of the most moving testimonies preserved in stone, for they bear the imprint of the unhappy passion and disillusioned power that were Michelangelo's destiny. He worked on these statues at a tragic period which witnessed the capture and sack of Rome by the Imperials and, under the pressure of Charles V, the end of the Republic and the return to Florence of second-rate Medici. In a stanza Michelangelo, also a great poet, puts these words into the mouth of the woman in whom he embodies Sleep and Night: 'Not to see, not to hear is a blessing in these times of infamy and shame. Do not wake me, I beg you . . . speak in a low voice . . .'.

Rarely did Michelangelo achieve the suggestive power in the face of *Dusk*, which he deliberately left unfinished. One is reminded of Rodin, but Rodin was a man of simple and vigorous passions, a stranger to the pride of the heights and the anguish of the depths which held the great Florentine sculptor in their grip. Speaking of Michelangelo, the Frenchman remarked, as if reluctantly: 'The most powerful genius of modern times celebrated the epic of the shadows, while the Ancients sang the epic of light.'

As you come out of the New Sacristy, you will find the Chapel of the Princes, situated behind the chancel of San Lorenzo. The construction of this luxurious octagonal edifice, covered with marble and rare stones, began in the early seventeenth century. At first rather mysteriously intended to house the Holy Sepulchre, which the Emir Farcadin had promised to bring to Florence, the chapel became the burial-place of the grand dukes; its different faces accommodate six porphyry tombs each surmounted by a bronze statue of the deceased: Cosimo I, Francesco I, Ferdinando I, Cosimo II, Ferdinando II and Cosimo III, names without glory but which ensured the continuity of the crown from the sixteenth to the eighteenth centuries. The crypt contains forty-five tombs of the Medici family; the central pillar contains the remains of Cosimo the Elder, the 'Father of the Country'.

The Palazzo Medici, which Cosimo the Elder commissioned Michelozzo to build in 1444, was the model for Florentine palaces of the Renaissance. Unfortunately, only two of its sides were finished and major modifications

THE LAURENTIAN LIBRARY, *founded by Cosimo the Elder in his private dwelling, was one of the first libraries in Europe to be opened to the educated public; it was considerably enriched by Lorenzo the Magnificent, who had a passion for books and manuscripts and after whom the library is named. Taken to Rome by a Medici Pope, Leo X, the library was presented to Florence by another Medici, Pope Clement VII, who commissioned Michelangelo to design an edifice suitable for the study and preservation of the documents. Michelangelo built the hall and the amazing staircase, thoroughly Baroque in inspiration; he drew up the plans for the main room, the inlaid ceiling and the twenty-eight desks which were to hold the illuminated manuscripts. His plans were used by Ammannati and Vasari, who continued the work.*
This famous library now contains ten thousand manuscripts. Among the most precious are some fragments of Tacitus, a fifth-century manuscript of Virgil, a sixth-century Syriac Bible, a copy of Boccaccio's 'The Decameron' dating from 1384, a copy of 'Horace' annotated by Petrarch, and the celebrated Pandects of Justinian (sixth century).
THE CLOISTER OF SAN LORENZO *adjoining the library was designed by Brunelleschi. A vast and graceful structure, this oasis of peace at the heart of the city was for a long time the refuge of stray cats.*

LAURENTIAN LIBRARY

were made in the seventeenth century by the Riccardi family. The palace, inhabited by the Medici for more than a hundred years, knew many glorious hours. It was here that the court of Lorenzo the Magnificent shone and that the future Pope Leo X and Catherine de' Medici spent their childhood. Emperors, kings, popes and most other great dignitaries of the fifteenth and sixteenth centuries were received here. All that remains of the palace's artistic treasures is the private chapel where in 1459, at the command of Piero the Gouty, Benozzo Gozzoli painted the frescoes that were to become famous. Three walls of the narrow chapel are decorated with the Journey of the Magi to Bethlehem, a fresco full of freshness and exotic splendour. The figures in the procession commemorate an event that had taken place in Florence thirty years earlier, the General Council summoned to reconcile the Church of the East and that of the West. The Council was presided over by Pope Eugenius IV. The Emperor of the East, John Palaeologus, and the patriarch of Constantinople, who were both present, represent two of the Magi in the painting; the third, youthful and dressed all in white, is the Medici heir Lorenzo, who was to become Lorenzo the Magnificent.

THE COURTYARD OF THE PALAZZO MEDICI-RICCARDI *by* MICHELOZZO; *stucco medallions by* BERTOLDO.

Near the Piazza San Marco and next to the university, which occupies the old stables of the grand dukes, stands the Academy of Fine Arts (Accademia di Belle Arti). Most of the works in the art gallery of the Academy are by Florentine and Sienese early masters, but it owes its celebrity to Michelangelo since it possesses the original of his *David* and most of his unfinished statues. The Casa Buonarroti, the house near Santa Croce where he lived, houses the works of his youth and those of lesser dimensions, such as the *Battle of the Centaurs*, the *Madonna of the Stairs* and the model for the façade of San Lorenzo.

In the gallery leading to the rotunda where the *David* stands, you will see against a background of admirable Flemish tapestries the marble and plaster preliminary versions of the *Slaves* intended for the tomb of Pope Julius II. This commission haunted Michelangelo for forty years and was the object of innumerable dealings with the Pope's heirs. The only elements of the grand project to reach completion were the two *Slaves* in the Louvre and the colossal *Moses* which stands alone under the Pope's sarcophagus in the church of St Peter's Chains in Rome. Yet these three marble statues would in themselves be sufficient for the glory of their sculptor. Even the preliminary versions in the Academy have a startling power; life springs from their unmodelled but already liberated forms. Other unfinished works, such as the *Pietà* from Palestrina and the statue of *St Matthew*, betray the strange lassitude which overcame Michelangelo when he was working – as if, disillusioned in his power, after having given proof of his ambition and his genius, he suddenly became aware of the absurdity of human creation.

Until 1873, when it was replaced by a copy, the celebrated statue of David stood near the entrance of the Palazzo Vecchio or Signoria. This was Michelangelo's first great work, bringing him glory at the age of thirty. Carved from a gigantic block of Carrara marble which had been abandoned after a first attempt, forty years earlier, by Agostino di Duccio, the robust body and the face showing courage and wrath are the symbols of Florence struggling for her liberty against powerful enemies. In fact, this hero, the embodiment of controlled strength, could as well be called Hercules or Augustus Caesar; it has been said that Michelangelo was the great artist that ancient Rome had lacked.

Once the years of his youthful triumphs were past Michelangelo, impelled by inordinate ambition and tortured by his frustrated dream, exhausted his great energy in a painful and endless struggle. He has been criticized for his love of the colossal and for a blind devotion to Antiquity which, it is suggested, precipitated the decline of Italian architecture and statuary towards coldness and artifice. But did he really corrupt Western art, as he is sometimes accused of doing? Surely, his genius merely gave concrete form to the inescapable forces of evolution. For thousands of years the artist had kept his personality out of his art, which had been the expression of a faith, a system of knowledge and a tradition. This was true even of Giotto and Brunelleschi, despite the originality of their genius. The time came when, in art as in other spheres, Man was to reveal his desire to express himself, for himself and through himself, thereby bringing about the destruction of a balance between Man and Nature. Yet, even if this need for personal expression imperilled the sincerity and purity of art, which was now at the mercy of the excesses of emotion and intention, it was part of the destiny of Man and, with him, was embarking on an uncertain but thrilling adventure.

Of all the squares in Florence the Piazza della Santissima Annunziata is the most elegant and the most faithful to the spirit of the Renaissance, spoilt only by the cars that clutter it. Arcades run along three sides of the square; the arcade of the Hospital of the Innocents (Ospedale degli Innocenti), one of Brunelleschi's masterpieces, faces that of the Brotherhood of the Servants of Mary (Confraternità dei Servi di Maria), which dates from the sixteenth century and is a replica of the first. The third arcade stands in front of the atrium decorated with frescoes by Andrea del Sarto, Baldovinetti, Pontormo and Rosso, which leads to the Church of Santissima Annunziata.

In the thirteenth century seven noblemen retired into solitude on Monte Senario, near Florence, to dedicate themselves to the Virgin Mary, founding the Order of the Servants of Mary under the Rule of St Augustine. In the darkest hours of the city's fratricidal struggles the Order was to wield a pacifying influence over Florence.

A thirteenth-century painting of the Annunciation, believed to be miraculous, brought the shrine great popularity. The Florentines have always had a special devotion to the Annunciation; in fact, until 1750, the New Year began in Florence on 25th March, the Feast of the Annunciation.

The church, enriched by donations, has lost its original design of the Quattrocento; its Baroque decoration is a rarity in Florentine religious architecture, whose chief characteristic is its sobriety.

far left *One of the twelve majolica medallions by* ANDREA DELLA ROBBIA *which decorate the* FAÇADE OF THE HOSPITAL OF THE INNOCENTS (above). *These 'bambini', all different in design and in their attitudes, were intended to stir the compassion of passers-by and encourage charitable gifts. There is an elegant inner courtyard and the church contains a beautiful 'Adoration of the Magi' by Ghirlandaio. The visitor will probably pass little bands of happy children, escorted by sisters who carry on the work of the oldest foundling children's home in Europe (it dates from 1421).*

left FOUNTAIN *by* PIETRO TACCA. *The same artist also completed the equestrian statue of Grand Duke Ferdinando I which stands on the square. The statue, which was begun by Giambologna, was cast in the bronze of cannon captured from the Berbers.*

p. 96

above ST JULIAN *by* ANDREA DEL CASTAGNO. *Detail of one of the two frescoes by Castagno discovered beneath later decorations. Anyone who would like to know more about this original and forceful artist should go to the monastery of Sant'Apollonia, which is not far away and contains several of his works, including the* Last Supper. *In the last room of the Uffizi Gallery there are also the full-length frescoes of famous persons, including Dante, Boccaccio and Petrarch, which are the first great paintings of lay figures.*

below THE PIAZZA SANTISSIMA ANNUNZIATA. *Engraving by Giuseppe Zocchi (1711–1767). At the far end, the church of SS. Annunziata and its atrium; to the right, the Hospital of the Innocents, the façade of which was designed by Brunelleschi; to the left, the Confraternità dei Servi di Maria.*

Zocchi's engravings are skilful and also of great documentary interest, for the buildings of Florence are represented as they appeared in the eighteenth century. This book contains photographs of several of them (embankments of the Arno, Duomo, Uffizi).

The monastery of San Marco, built in the thirteenth century by the monks of the Order of St Sylvester, was occupied during the Quattrocento by the Dominicans of Fiesole. Cosimo the Elder instructed Michelozzo to enlarge and embellish the modest original edifice. The cloister bears the name of S. Antonino, the great archbishop of Florence in the fifteenth century, who was prior of San Marco and opposed the oligarchic power of the Medici, in spite of Cosimo's liberality. The same Dominican intransigence inspired Girolamo Savonarola, whose eloquence stunned the people of Florence: 'During his sermons,' wrote a contemporary, 'the church resounded with weeping and lamentations.' His moral and political authority soon became considerable. When Piero II de' Medici fled on the approach of Louis XII, king of France, he was elected political head of the city. Some have chosen to see in Savonarola the scourge of God, a fanatical enemy of the arts, of freedom, flowers and love. In fact, this ascetic was a noble-hearted and high-minded man, the friend of Pico della Mirandola and of many humanists. On his deathbed Lorenzo the Magnificent, who had often been the object of his attacks, asked for his blessing.

Savonarola, prior of San Marco, embodied the old scholastic ideal, the union of civic, moral and religious virtues. The constitution which he gave Florence reflected his ideals of civic dignity and spiritual aspiration. He deprived the Signoria of the right to condemn a citizen to exile or death without appeal.

The times were unjust and cruel. To preserve their power, the Medici had encouraged demagogy, privilege and corruption. In Florence, gambling, debauchery and sodomy were rife. Street hooligans robbed passers-by or killed them with stones. At first the new régime was well received by the Florentines, partly in a mood of religious enthusiasm and partly because they felt the need for order, but they soon tired of this austere life. Violently attacked by Savonarola, the new Pope, Alexander VI Borgia, who according to Guicciardini was 'obscene in his morals, without integrity, faith or religion, of insatiable cupidity and ambition, and more than barbarous in his cruelty', excommunicated him and plotted his downfall. Pronounced a 'heretic and schismatic', Savonarola, with two of his disciples, was sentenced to death, strangled and burnt on the Piazza della Signoria on 23rd May 1498. His preaching and example were to leave a profound imprint on the consciences of the Florentines.

S. Antonio entrusted the decoration of the monastery of San Marco to one of his friars, Fra Giovanni da Fiesole, later called 'Blessed Angelico' ('Beato Angelico'). The pictures and frescoes were intended to encourage meditation among the Dominican friars. The great Crucifixion in the cloister, with the figure of St Dominic, stands out against a deep blue background, a severe invitation to spiritual contemplation. In a lunette above the chapter-room St Dominic is seen showing the book of the order's rule and the cord of discipline. The hostelry, converted into a museum, contains some fine paintings by Fra Angelico: the *Coronation of the Virgin*, the *Last Judgement*, the *Madonna and Star* and the *Deposition*. Despite their spirituality, the freshness of the colours and the charm of the compositions are delightful. The severity of the frescoes here makes way for a different kind of testimony to the glory of God: the wondrous quality of his Creation. One feels that this artist of simple, happy faith was touched by the message of St Francis of Assisi and shared his brotherly love

THE ENTOMBMENT *by* FRA ANGELICO *(1387–1455) and his famous* ANNUNCIATION *on the first floor of the monastery, greeting the monks as they returned to their cells.*

FRA ANGELICO *occupies a special place among the painters of the Quattrocento. He was a true saint, famous for his modesty and extremely sensitive (it is said that he used to weep as he painted the Crucifixion); he was the prior of San Marco, but declined the bishopric of Florence.*
The grace and spirituality of this artist seem to illumine his composition and to irradiate the dazzling colours of his palette. At the same time, he is one of the artists in whom the juxtaposition of the Middle Ages and the Renaissance is most clearly discernible. His paintings still reflect certain Gothic structures, the brocades and opaque golds dear to the Sienese artists of the thirteenth century. And yet, this contemporary of Masaccio and Uccello was not insensitive to his epoch. In the freshness of his colouring and a sense of space and movement which is more true than in the works of Giotto, Fra Angelico was also an innovator. He painted the first real landscapes of Florentine art, scenes marked by a concern for precision which in no way diminishes the charm of his work.

for animals and Nature.

At the top of the staircase leading to the cells is the delicate and famous *Annunciation*. The narrow white cells, arranged on each side of long corridors covered with timber-work, are decorated with frescoes illustrating New Testament themes. The frescoes of Fra Angelico – the *Transfiguration*, the *Coronation of the Virgin* and the *Descent into Limbo* – have a deep spirituality and sober but expressive colours. The cells of the novices contain more modest frescoes on the same theme: Jesus on the cross, bruised and bleeding, the symbol of monastic meditation and penitence.

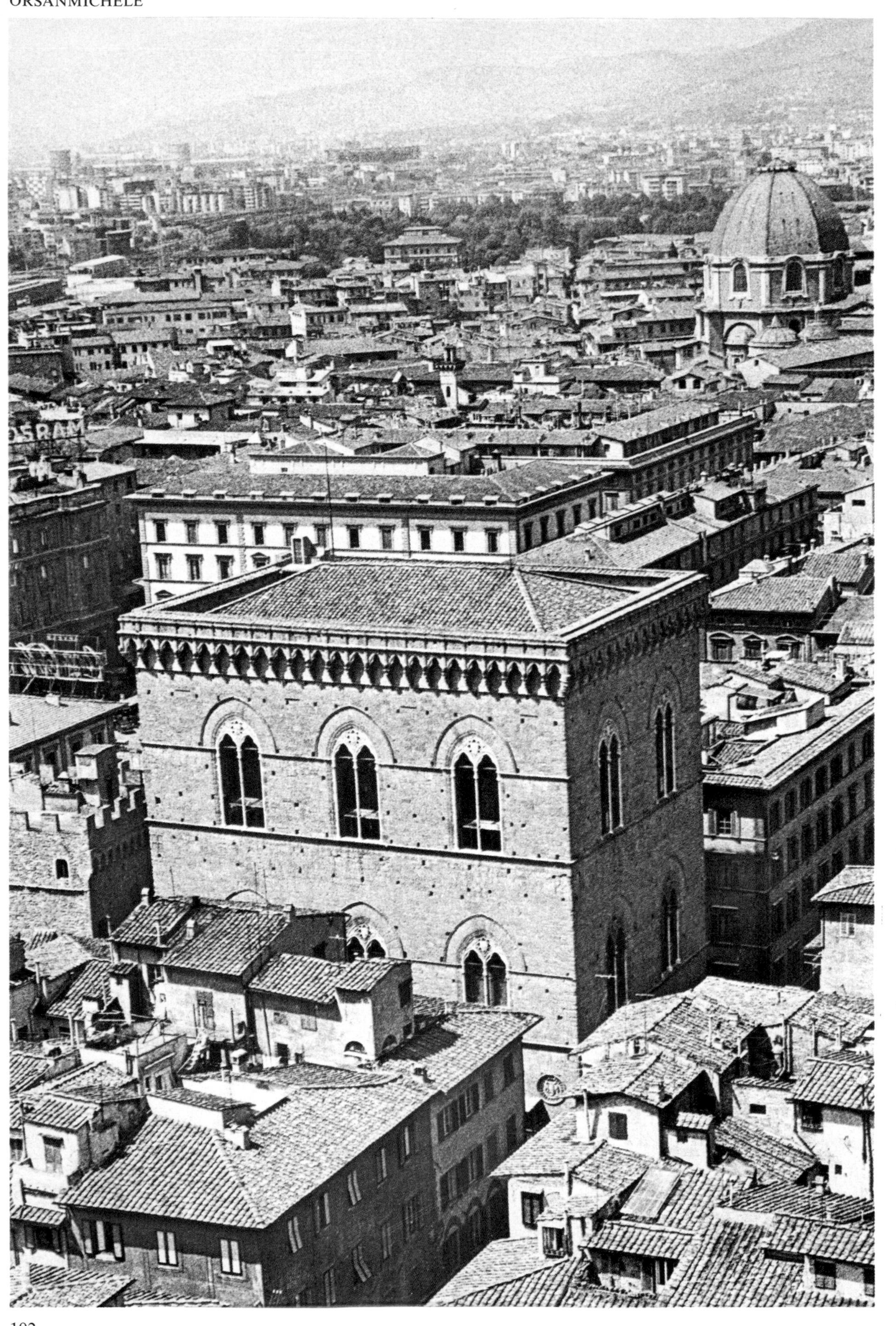

ORSANMICHELE, *its square mass resembling a skilfully chiselled Gothic reliquary, is one of Florence's most interesting monuments, for it is both a civic and a religious edifice. It stands on the site of a Carolingian monastery, San Michele in Orto, after which it is named. At first it was a corn market or loggia and the upper part served as a granary to provide against famine. One of the pillars was decorated with a painting of the Virgin which was said to be miraculous. In 1348 the Black Death ravaged Florence and many of its inhabitants bequeathed their possessions to the charitable Company of Orsanmichele. In the following year, a popular uprising drove out Gautier de Brienne, duke of Athens, who had been invited to govern Florence. It was decided to honour the Virgin and St Anne in thanksgiving by transforming the loggia into a church. Simone Talenti, who*

had assisted in its construction, walled up the arcades with a light curtain of carved stone and wide stained-glass windows. In niches hollowed in the outer pillars were placed statues of the patron saints of the various 'arti' or guilds of Florence, which had played an important role during the difficult days of plague and rebellion.
Fourteen statues or groups of statues thus bear striking testimony to the sculpture of the Quattrocento, with works by Ghiberti, Nanno di Banco, Donatello and Verrochio. The best-known is Donatello's 'St George', patron of the armourers' guild (the original is in the Bargello Museum).
In the church of Orsanmichele, the celebrated marble tabernacle encrusted with mosaics of gold and lapis lazuli, the work of Andrea Orcagna (1308–1359), was made to hold the miraculous picture of the Virgin; this painting was destroyed by fire and replaced with the present painting of the Virgin by Bernardo Daddi. Even if this huge tabernacle seems a little overloaded in its execution, it is a masterpiece of sculpture and the bas-reliefs and medallions are of rare delicacy.
Orsanmichele is linked by a little stone footbridge to the Palazzo dell'Arte della Lana, which was largely restored in the nineteenth century. The 'Arte della Lana', the wool guild, was one of the wealthiest, with the 'Arte della Seta' (silk guild) and the 'Arte di Calimala' (guild of the dressers and dyers of imported cloths). The 'Arti Maggiori', or greater guilds, which were to play a decisive role in the government of Florence, also included the guilds of the judges and notaries, the bankers, the physicians and pharmacists, and the furriers. The 'Arti Minori' or lesser guilds comprised some fifteen smaller organizations: the butchers, shoemakers, tanners, oil-merchants, smiths, armourers, innkeepers, etc. Their number varied from time to time; Lorenzo the Magnificent reduced them to five in order to control them more effectively.

above *The famous* FOUNTAIN OF THE 'PORCELLINO', *a copy of a bronze by Pietro Tacca. Stroking the snout of this boar is traditionally supposed to bring good luck and, for the tourist, the certainty of returning to Florence one day.*

right *The cry of the water-melon vendor, 'È sangue! È sangue!', might seem a little extravagant, but in fact the flesh of a good melon should be blood-red.*

below THE LOGGIA OF THE NEW MARKET *dates from the sixteenth century; it was thus named to distinguish it from the old market which was destroyed in the preceding century and which occupied the centre of the city, where the vast and unsightly 'Piazza della Repubblica' now lies.*

p. 105

above THE NEW MARKET, *formerly the meeting-place of the greater guilds and the silk and wool trades, is now occupied by flower-sellers and vendors of handicraft articles. Florence is the city of flowers and owes its name to them; the lily, its emblem, is the true symbol of its elegance.*

below *Another colourful part of Florence: the* ARCO DI SAN PIETRO.

MARKET

5

SANTA TRINITÀ – PALAZZO PITTI – BOBOLI GARDENS – THE BELVEDERE – ARCETRI AND THE HILLS OF FLORENCE – SAN MINIATO.

The visitor will find himself returning frequently to the banks of the Arno, for it is here that all the changing colours of day and season – gold, white, pink, mauve, or grey – are reflected in the old stones of the city.

Although its back faces on to the river, the Church of San Frediano in Cestello, with its light cupola, presents a graceful appearance; it dates from the seventeenth century and its name commemorates the old Cistercian monastery founded by the white-robed monks of St Bernard of Clairvaux.

The Ponte Santa Trinità leads to the celebrated Via Tornabuoni, the most elegant street in Florence since the fifteenth century. First you pass between the two military palaces which guard its entrance; the crenellated Palazzo Spini-Ferroni faces on to the Arno. Further along, on the left, stands the narrow Baroque façade of the Church of Santa Trinità, designed by Buontalenti at the end of the sixteenth century. The interior architecture is in the bare Gothic style of the Cistercians. This was the first church in Florence of the monks of Vallombrosa, an order founded in 1036 by S. Giovanni Gualberto, reformer of the Benedictine Rule and of the morals of the clergy. The order had an important influence on the religious and civic life of Florence, and its monks, whose austerity and dignity were exemplary, often sat on the councils of the Republic.

The Sassetti Chapel, in the right arm of the transept of Santa Trinità, is typical of the lavish family chapels of the Renaissance. Its frescoes, which are among Ghirlandaio's finest achievements, illustrate the life of St Francis, the patron saint of the donor. In one of the frescoes Pope Honorius is seen confirming the Rule of St Francis. The setting is the Piazza della Signoria and the Loggia dei Lanzi; to the right, by the side of Francesco Sassetti, is a striking portrait of Lorenzo the Magnificent. At the bottom of the painting, climbing some steps, appears the poet and humanist Agnolo Poliziano, tutor of Lorenzo's children; the youngest child, Giuliano, the future duke of Nemours, walks beside him and is followed by his brothers, Piero, who succeeded his father as ruler of Florence, and Giovanni, the future Pope Leo X. Behind them are Luigi Pulci, the author of an astonishing burlesque tale, *Morgante*, which foreshadows Rabelais, and the canon Matteo Franco. The presence of these humanists with his children shows the atmosphere in which Lorenzo had chosen to live.

Francesco Sassetti had been appointed as head of the Medici companies by Cosimo a few years before the latter's death. Piero the Gouty and Lorenzo the Magnificent left the family affairs to him; consequently, he bore a heavy share of responsibility for the decline of the financial power of the Medici. There were eight companies in 1459, but on Lorenzo's death in 1492 there were only three. The London company closed in 1472 because Edward IV had been unable to repay the loans contracted during the Wars of the Roses. The Bruges company disappeared with Charles the Bold, duke of Burgundy, who owed it sixty thousand ducats. The Milan company merely served to impoverish the Medici by enriching the Sforza family. In the second half of the fifteenth century Europe suffered an enormous economic recession. Nevertheless, it is true that Francesco Sassetti did not choose his managers wisely and did not supervise them. Having amassed a fortune for himself, he followed his master's example and devoted most of his time to the delights of humanism.

Wealth had brought the Medici to power, and only power was to save them from bankruptcy.

Originally peasants from the Arno Valley, then craftsmen and merchants, the Medici had risen to eminence through the world of business at a time when large-scale commerce was beginning to grow and when a new social class was emerging, relegating the feudal nobility and its heroic values to the past. The arena of their commercial activity was indeed privileged. In 1253 Florence had struck its first gold coin, the florin bearing the lily emblem; by the fourteenth century, with the practice of bills of exchange which it had introduced, it was the leading financial city of Europe.

GIOVANNI DI BICCI

Giovanni di Bicci de' Medici (1360–1429), an unobtrusive but active merchant of the *Arte della lana* (the wool guild) and a country cousin of the Medici family, which had been famous in Florence since the thirteenth century, was elected *Gonfaloniere di Giustizia* at the age of sixty. His sense of justice and his modesty and benevolence quickly earned him great popularity among the lower orders, the *popolo minuto*. He strove to defend their interests, lowering the duties on salt, having taxes recorded on an official register, the *catasto*, which was open to all, and resisting the aristocratic and bellicose ambitions of his own social class, the *ottimati*, the great families of merchants and bankers such as the Albizzi, the Capponi and the Rucellai. Unostentatious but generous, he commissioned Brunelleschi to prepare the plans for the Church of San Lorenzo, which was to become the parish church of the Medici; at the time of the competition for the cupola of the Duomo, displaying an open-mindedness rare at this period, he asked his managers to seek the candidature of Flemish, French and German architects. In 1397 he had founded the Medici bank and, to avoid the disasters suffered by the great Florentine bankers of the fourteenth century, the Bardi, the Peruzzi and the Buonaccorsi, he had given the foreign branches the character of independent subsidiary companies. Under his direction and that of his son, Cosimo, the family enterprise soon became one of the most successful in Florence.

Cosimo the Elder, forty years old on the death of his father, assumed control of the family fortune. The *Arte del cambio* – loans at interest, exchange operations, the utilization and repayment of deposits lodged by the Papacy, by prelates and by wealthy merchants – was henceforth the principal activity of the Medici companies. The wool trade with England and Castile, the finishing of unbleached cloths from France and the Netherlands, and the monopoly of the alum which was essential for fixing dyes, all of which had contributed to the prosperity of Florence and of the Medici family, now became secondary activities, although the varied needs of a luxury clientele continued to be met – for example, the provision of Circassian slaves, and of boy sopranos for the choir of St John Lateran.

Cosimo had travelled throughout Europe and had an excellent knowledge of the money market. He quickly gathered numerous associates around him, organizing a group of committed supporters who were to make his political fortune. An uncrowned king, Cosimo never held an official title in thirty years of rule except for that of 'Gonfalonier of Justice', which he bore for only six months. But he understood perfectly the hypocritical game of Florentine democracy – pretending to give the people power without ever really doing so.

The Florentines hated noble titles and privileges, but they admired success and respected money. Beneath the appearance of good-natured simplicity fostered by Cosimo, money assumed control of Florence. His secret was never to let his power be seen; while his henchmen held the Signoria in check, he showered it with honours and tokens of respect. True to his plebian origins and to the family tradition, Cosimo defended the cause of the populace against the great families, but without hesitating to seek the co-operation of those that could serve his purpose. A skilful demagogue, he humoured the mob with frequent public entertainments – processions, carnivals, contests of wild beasts – and used arbitrary taxation to ruin his enemies. He knew better than anyone how to play with assemblies and obtain, by pressure or by trickery, a majority for the decisions he wanted.

COSIMO THE ELDER

After an ill-fated war against Lucca, Cosimo was accused by Rinaldo Albizzi of wishing 'to raise himself above all others and reduce the people to servitude' and was first imprisoned, then exiled; on his return he singled out his enemies and had them banished in vast numbers. When the need arose he would arrange assassinations, as everyone else did, but did not practise violence of the kind associated with the brutal tyrants of the Renaissance – Sforza, Malatesta, and Ferrante of Aragon, the monster who was king of Naples. Viewed in the context of the period, the highly favourable judgement of the chronicler Commines, who saw Cosimo wielding 'a kind and gentle authority, as befits a free city', is correct.

A man of a positive, practical disposition, Cosimo did not hesitate to reverse Florence's traditional alliances and join with Sforza, duke of Milan, and the Pope against Venice and Naples. A few years before his death, he drew closer to France and its new king, Louis XI. Rather curiously, there were many points of resemblance, both physical and moral, between Cosimo and the king of France. Both concealed their greed and ambition beneath an appearance of modesty. They were calculating men who were always ready to compromise, and preferred intrigue to force: they could not count on success in armed conflict, but were confident of their own cleverness. They both liked to live simply and dressed like merchants. If Cosimo's power was less far-reaching than that of Louis XI, who by the end of the fifteenth century was to make France the leading nation of Europe, he had the advantage of a culture which, although rare at this time, was traditional in his family. He had listened to the Greek philosopher Gemistos Plethon and encouraged the young Marsilio Ficino in his Neo-Platonic studies. All the major artists of the time had worked for him: Brunelleschi, Donatello, Verrocchio, Michelozzo, Alberti, Uccello, Castagno and Filippo Lippi.

Although he would probably not have liked the title of 'Pater Patriae' ('Father of the Country') which his fellow citizens bestowed on him when he died, Cosimo deserved it. If, as Machiavelli wrote, 'one owes the people only results', the results of his government were many and brilliant: commercial and financial prosperity, wonderful monuments, magnificent entertainments, but also schools, hospitals, help for the needy, the organization of savings for housing the populace and the provision of dowries for poor girls. All this activity was illumined by that golden light of hope and glory that shone over the first half of the Quattrocento.

PIERO THE GOUTY

Since Giovanni de' Medici, a radiant and popular figure, had died two years before his father, Cosimo was succeeded in 1464 by his second son Piero, called 'the Gouty' because of his infirmity. Piero showed much skill in facing the financial and political problems that confronted him in abundance, in particular the uprising led by Luca Pitti, a former associate of his father. He died in 1469, leaving two sons: Lorenzo, aged twenty-one, and Giuliano, four years younger.

Glory and renown thrust themselves upon Lorenzo the Magnificent, making him the prince of the Renaissance and its symbol. His physique revealed his peasant origins: like Giovanni di Bicci and Cosimo, his grandfather, he had rough features, a long, drooping nose and rather thick lips, but he also had their energetic chin and alert eyes.

For his contemporaries, whose fulsome praise was not always disinterested, he was 'the ideal man', the masterpiece of human harmony of which the humanist educators dreamed. His teachers had been the greatest intellects of his time and his mother, Laura Tornabuoni, had watched over his religious and moral education. He possessed an irresistible charm. He was simple and yet refined. Endowed with physical vitality and agility, a good horseman and a great hunter, he thirsted for knowledge, and was a connoisseur of the arts and a lover of Nature. An amiable and kindly person, he also knew, when necessary, how to give orders and command obedience.

LORENZO THE MAGNIFICENT

Lorenzo enjoyed immense popularity with the people. He enjoyed carnivals and organized them himself. He deserved this fine compliment from Machiavelli: 'Raised and nurtured with his fellow citizens, he governed them with such familiarity that they regarded it as a kindness.' He was, moreover, a good father; his wife, the Roman princess Clarice Orsini, gave him ten children of whom he was very fond.

Although Lorenzo was an adroit politician and diplomat, wrote Latin and composed verse in the language of Dante, he knew nothing about business matters and his government was to witness the dramatic decline of the Medici bank. The progressive shortage of money that he experienced partly explains why he was not as enterprising a patron of the arts as his grandfather Cosimo. He took little interest in architecture and, though he invited the young Michelangelo to his table and encouraged painters and sculptors, he provided few commissions and allowed Botticelli and the Pollaiuolo brothers to leave for Rome, Verrocchio for Venice and Leonardo for Milan. Above all, he loved gold and silver work and other rare and precious objects. His tastes were literary rather than artistic. Although he does not appear to have been an assiduous student at the Platonic Academy that had formed around Marsilio Ficino, he received in the gardens of Careggi its most eminent members, Luigi Pulci, Agnolo Poliziano and Pico della Mirandola, perhaps the richest and most original of these intellects, together with an assorted collection of artists, doctors, businessmen and churchmen who shared the same humanist preoccupations. Lorenzo's poetic work is not of much interest in itself;

like the Florentine literature of the period, it follows the ancient authors too slavishly. But its surprising diversity is quite revealing of the spirit of the times: there are pastoral poems, moderately licentious carnival songs, a prayer based on a psalm of David, and hymns of praise inspired by the Passion of Christ which contain this moving cry: 'Abandon the poor paths you have trodden and turn your gaze to the eternal beauties.'

In fact, at a time when painting and sculpture were radiating with richness and novelty, Lorenzo, in concerning himself with poetry and literature, was devoting his energies to the domain in which the Quattrocento showed least originality and invention.

Lorenzo was a shrewd and practical politician. Clashing with Pope Sixtus IV because his eight-year-old son had been refused a cardinal's hat, he only narrowly escaped death in the Pazzi conspiracy in which his brother, Giuliano, was killed. When the papal legate, who had been involved in the plot, had been hanged, Lorenzo went to stay for several months with the redoubtable king of Naples, the Pope's ally, succeeding in obtaining the king's neutrality and then in securing peace through his intercession. A few years earlier, in 1472, he had been responsible for a less glorious event, the bloody sacking of Volterra, although that city was the ally of Florence and had only been defending its lawful rights.

Although he already controlled the various councils, Lorenzo decided in 1480 to modify the institutions of Florence. He arranged that the *priori* would be elected by a council of seventy members chosen by himself and that the various powers would be exercised by a reduced council answerable solely to himself. The people accepted this violation of its rights with strange docility, perhaps because, as Guicciardini wrote, 'if it was no longer free, it felt that it could not have found a better or a more likeable despot'. It was in political glory and financial disaster that Lorenzo the Magnificent ended his career in 1492. He was forty-two years old; he died young, as heroes should. In fact, the last decade of his government had marked the beginning of a grave crisis – moral, political and financial. The Renaissance had seen the enthusiasm of the first humanists turn to disillusionment: after the vigour of Donatello, the melancholy of Botticelli; after the naïve faith of Fra Angelico, the imprecations of Savonarola.

If Florence and the Medici had together known glory and prosperity, their happy association was finally terminated in 1529 when a Medici Pope, Clement VII, though a victim of the sack of Rome by the Imperials, launched the troops of Charles V against his native city, which for the second time had just driven out a Medici. After a siege of eight months Florence was taken; this was a disaster both for its population and for its works of art, a disaster which Clement VII prolonged by terrible reprisals.

The return of the Medici sounded the death-knell of political liberties and of the wonderful collective adventure that had been the Quattrocento. Henceforth, the Medici were ruling princes, living amid the splendour of courts and seeking the prestige of alliances. The spirit of enterprise and simplicity made way for official pomp.

The Palazzo Medici on the Via Larga was not grand enough for cousins of the Pope or the brother of the queen of France. The Medici chose and enlarged a more ambitious dwelling, the Palazzo Pitti. As you come out of the Via Guicciardini, where the palace of the same name was the birthplace of Francesco Guicciardini, the great Florentine historian of the sixteenth century, you will see the vast, severe façade of the Palazzo Pitti.

Luca Pitti belonged to an extremely wealthy family of older origins than the Medici themselves. This successful banker, the associate of Cosimo and frequently *Gonfaloniere* of the Commune, commissioned Brunelleschi to prepare the plans for the palace in 1440, but its construction did not begin until 1460. Ten years later Luca Pitti, involved in a conspiracy against Piero the Gouty, was compelled to make the *amende honorable* and sell his palace. The original building, faithful to the Quattrocento conception of a square plan with inner courtyard, was already of unusually large dimensions. Unlike the earlier Medici, who had considered Brunelleschi's plans too extravagant for their palace and preferred the more modest design of Michelozzo, the new rulers were clearly anxious to display their wealth. Marie de' Medici spent her childhood here and was influenced by it when she had the Luxembourg Palace built in Paris. In the seventeenth and especially the eighteenth centuries, under the grand dukes of the Lorraine family, the palace assumed its present imposing appearance as a result of frequent additions, which included an extension of the façade and two new wings.

The palace today houses two excellent museums, the Galleria Palatina and the Museo degli Argenti (Museum of Silverware).

The Galleria Palatina, containing the paintings which formed the private collection of the grand dukes, is one of the finest exhibitions of portraits in the world. Raphael, who was the protégé of the Medici Pope Leo X, for whom he decorated the rooms and galleries of the Vatican, is here represented by eleven paintings, some of which are famous, such as the *Madonna of the Chair* or the *Veiled Woman*, and all of which are admirable; these pictures are the triumph of harmony, the summit of sixteenth-century classical art. Fourteen paintings by Titian are also exhibited. Indeed, for anyone interested in these two supreme artists, this collection of pictures is of great importance. There are also some beautiful portraits by Ghirlandaio, Botticelli, van Dyck and Tintoretto, and two excellent compositions, the *Concert*, said to be an early work of Titian, and the *Consequences of War*, a brilliant and passionate allegory by Rubens.

On the ground floor the Museo degli Argenti, comprising four sumptuous rooms, contains the precious objects of which the Medici were discriminating collectors; ivories, gems, gold and silver plate, gilded and jewelled cups, vases and ewers of crystal or hard stone (jasper, onyx, agate).

right *The third room of the* MUSEO DEGLI ARGENTI, *decorated with 'trompe-l'œil' frescoes by Colonna and Mitelli (seventeenth century). In the centre, a very rare German ebony cupboard of the seventeenth century, acquired by Grand Duke Ferdinando II.*

p. 114
THE DUKE OF NORFOLK, *also known as* THE MAN WITH GREEN EYES, *by* TITIAN *(1490–1576).*

THE VEILED WOMAN *by* RAPHAEL *(1483–1520). It is sometimes suggested that this is a portrait of 'La Fornarina', the baker's daughter whom Raphael loved and for whom he wrote his sonnets; but the 'Fornarina' of the Barberini Gallery in Rome, who wears a bracelet engraved with Raphael's name, is not the same woman. Which of the two is really the baker's daughter?*

below *From left to right: a shell mounted as a chalice from the treasure of the archbishops of Salzburg (sixteenth century) and purchased by Ferdinando III; a lapis-lazuli flask designed by Bernardo Buontalenti (grand-ducal workshops of the sixteenth century); thirteenth-century bowl with lid, of Venetian jasper, made for Lorenzo the Magnificent whose sigla 'Laur. Med.' is engraved in the stone; jasper bowl in the shape of a hydra, encrusted with pearls and decorated with a gold figure of Hercules.*

It was Cosimo I who, in 1549, commissioned Niccolò Pericoli, called 'IL TRIBOLO', *to design the famous* BOBOLI GARDENS, *which occupy the slope of the hill behind the palace. The irregular configuration of the ground precluded the geometric precision which the architect had applied to the villa of Castello, the first example of the 'Italian garden'. Though arranged in terraces and perspectives, the gardens have a more natural appearance: cypresses, holm oaks, umbrella pines, box trees and rose laurels line the avenues on which Roman or Neo-Classical statues stand.*

The grotto designed by Buontalenti, opposite the entrance of the Palazzo Pitti, is decorated with shells and stalactites and contains a graceful Venus emerging from the water, by Giambologna; it is a pity that this grotto is in such a neglected state.

The huge amphitheatre opens on to the majestic inner courtyard of the Palace and the 'Artichoke Fountain' which stands in its centre. From the top of the gardens an avenue of cypresses, the 'Viottolone', leads down to the Piazzale dell'Isolotto, in the middle of which there is an island with orange and lemon trees and the OCEAN FOUNTAIN *by Giambologna. At one time, the gardens also included an aviary, a fish-pond and a menagerie.*

It was largely in crime and vice that the Medici of the sixteenth and seventeenth centuries were to reveal their personalities. Allied with the royal families of Austria and France, they regarded themselves as princes by divine right and fleeced their people by the imposition of excessive taxes. Yet nearly all the reigning Medici showed in one way or another their interest in the arts and the sciences.

Francesco I collected a large number of pictures; he developed a passion for chemistry and mineralogy. Ferdinando I had a special liking for ancient statues and for music. In 1600 Jacopo Peri's *Eurydice*, considered the first opera in the history of music, was performed in the Palazzo Pitti. Ferdinando II experimented with the growing of the mulberry tree and the potato, and, rather curiously, tried to introduce camel-breeding into Tuscany. Cosimo II, fascinated by astrology, became the enthusiastic patron of Galileo. On the other hand, Cosimo III, a violent and tyrannical man, could only ape the splendour and authoritarianism of Louis XIV; his son, Giovanni Gastone, an extravagant person and something of a drunkard, found himself, three years before his death, deprived of his crown by the Treaty of Vienna, which awarded it by way of compensation to the duke of Lor-

raine, the future husband of Maria Theresa of Austria (he had been obliged to cede his duchy to Stanislas Leczinski, father-in-law of Louis XV). Except for the brief Napoleonic interlude, the House of Lorraine was to rule the grand duchy of Tuscany from 1735 to 1859, when the *Risorgimento* drove Francesco II, a benevolent and liberal prince, from Florence.

The well-proportioned fortress of the Belvedere, which overlooks the Boboli Gardens, was built in 1590 at the request of Ferdinando I, from plans prepared by Buontalenti according to the rules of military architecture. The graceful little palace that crowns the fortifications was intended as a refuge for the grand ducal family in the event of popular uprisings.

From the terraces of the Belvedere there is a magnificent view of Florence and the surrounding hills, from San Miniato to Monte Oliveto. The visitor should sit down and watch the stones of the city sparkling in the setting sun, allowing himself to absorb the unison of Nature and the works of Man. At night the illuminations emphasize the geometric architecture of the military edifices, while lower down, in its dark jewel-case, the city shimmers with thousands of lights.

Nowhere does the union of Man and Nature manifest itself with such grace and brilliance as on the hills of Florence. One understands why the chief concern of the Florentine artists was to express this wonderful harmony which surrounded them.

You should set off on foot for a walk of two to three hours, going up the Via San Lorenzo, an old road that has preserved its charm and tranquillity; amid the foliage of olive trees, cypresses and magnolias, it winds between two walls behind which lie gardens and fields, villas and old peasant houses. This was the world of the painter Ottone Rosai, a self-willed artist who, like his contemporary Utrillo, understood the language of simple surfaces like these walls. On the way you pass the little Church of San Leonardo; then you cross the Viale dei Colli, climb the hill of Arcetri, and come to the delightful village of Pian dei Giullari, where you will glimpse the medieval outline of the Torre del Gallo and several villas, including the house where Galileo died; from here two roads lead to two beautiful country churches, Santa Margherita a Montici and San Michele a Ripaldi. You can then go down an enchanting little lane called the Via del Giramonte. On the way to San Miniato, if you have chosen the right time of day, you will probably only meet a few children playing, a woman in black and a sleeping dog.

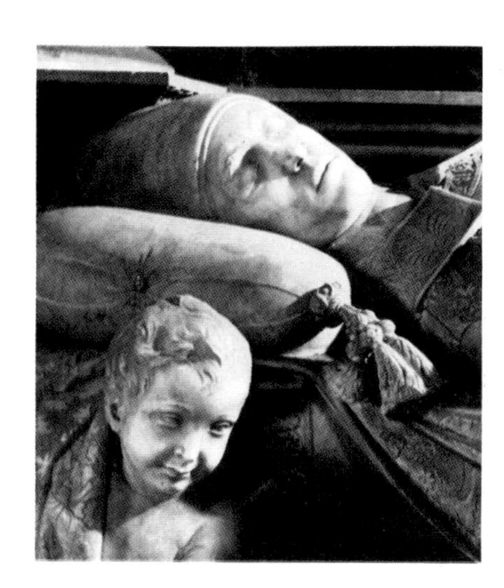

After passing through a bastion in the fortifications erected by Michelangelo for the defence of Florence against the Imperial army, you come to the façade of San Miniato, the oldest and the most moving church in Tuscany. Its construction began in 1014, financed with the gifts of the Emperor Henry II, the protector and friend of the bishop Hildebrand. This is Romanesque architecture at its most graceful and restrained. The lower and older part of the façade is even more strikingly simple than the upper part. Here is the very essence of the sobriety and harmony typical of Florentine religious architecture.

The interior is built on the three levels characteristic of Romanesque churches: the sombre crypt with its forest of columns; the huge nave, warm and welcoming with its marble facing and its roof of polychrome wood; and the raised chancel, reserved for the monks and separated from the nave by a handsome partition-wall of inlaid marble.

The church has two beautiful Renaissance chapels. One, designed by Michelozzo and with a ceiling by Luca della Robbia, contained the wooden crucifix of S. Giovanni Gualberto. The other chapel, on which the Pollaiuolo brothers, Luca della Robbia and Baldovinetti worked, has a remarkable tomb by Antonio Rossellino – the sarcophagus of Cardinal James of Portugal, who died in Florence. The design of this chapel presents a beautifully unified whole.

You can walk further over the hills to the south of Florence, if you have the energy; or, alternatively, you can go by car or bus. The Carthusian monastery, or Certosa of Galluzzo, lies only seven kilometres from the city; its buildings, with the church and the sixteen houses of the monks almost forming a single mass, are set in lovely countryside. The monastery was founded in 1341 by an enterprising Florentine, Niccolò Acciaiuoli, a friend of Petrarch and Boccaccio, who had made his fortune at the court of the king of Naples. Acciaiuoli wanted to create not only a citadel of faith, but also a centre of European culture. Unfortunately, this idea, which seems so appropriate to modern times, was never put into effect. The monks of the Order of St Bruno established the severe rule of the Carthusians; they were succeeded by the Cistercians, who do not practise obligatory silence, and so today the monastery is no longer isolated from the outside world. The buildings were modified over the centuries, but without much taste. They are, however, worth a visit: the church has a beautiful pavement and the main cloister, converted into a garden with a marble well in the centre, is surrounded by a graceful arcade decorated with terracotta medallions from the della Robbia workshop.

A few kilometres from Galluzzo, in the heart of the Chianti region with its hills and its valleys covered with vines, olive trees and pines, stands the Villa I Collazzi, a dazzling mass of white amid the dark tapering cypresses. The villa, the original plans of which are supposed to have been designed by Michelangelo, is both rustic and elegant, and reflects the tradition of rural simplicity that Michelozzo had established with the first Medicean villas at Trebbio and Fiesole. Volume, lines and planes are balanced in the manner of Brunelleschi. This same rather severe grace, which is also full of freshness, can be found in the façade of the church at Impruneta, a pretty and old little town that lies near by and offers a superb view over the hills of Chianti.

Impruneta is a delightful name. At the end of September a colourful harvest festival is held here. From 15th to 18th October there is the St Luke Fair, the horse and mule market once famous throughout Europe. Jacques Callot, the seventeenth-century French artist, made a series of engravings of the fair and the Venetian, Domenico Tiepolo, visited it several times to draw the asses, horses and mules.

6

PALAZZO STROZZI – PALAZZO DAVANZATI – PALAZZO RUCELLAI – SANTA MARIA NOVELLA.

Palla Strozzi, an active and enlightened patron of the arts, commissioned the plans for this palace, the most majestic in Florence, from Benedetto da Maiano. Built from 1489 to 1507, it combines all the features of the fifteenth-century Florentine palace: cubic in form, imposing and warlike with its facing of massive stones whose volume and relief diminish towards the cornice. Its simplicity is characteristic of Florence which, though so near to Carrara, preferred rusticated stone to marble. The square inner courtyard is severe but elegant, with a portico in the antique style. It contains lamp-holders and lanterns by Niccolò Grosso, the great master-blacksmith.

Since the end of the thirteenth century the Strozzi family, originally merchants of the 'Arte di Calimala' and then bankers, had enjoyed a success similar to that of the Medici, sometimes in association with them, sometimes their rivals. The power of the Strozzi alarmed the wealthy merchants of the 'popolo grasso' and they were exiled by the Signoria, like Cosimo the Elder a few years later. They settled in Lyon, and continued to amass great riches. Filippo Strozzi, who had supported the return of the Medici in 1531, gathered round him a number of great families hostile to the authoritarianism of Grand Duke Cosimo I. His son, Piero Strozzi, raised an army but was defeated in 1537. The ring-leaders were executed. Thereafter, the Strozzi, the Albizzi and several other families disappeared from the political scene.

COURTYARD OF THE PALAZZO DAVANZATI

PALAZZO GIANFIGLIAZZI

PALAZZO GIANFIGLIAZZI. *This palace was both a family residence and a fortress. When necessary, wooden bridges were suspended between the towers. The 'primo popolo' decided that the height of these fortress-towers, which facilitated intrigues and factions, should be reduced to nineteen metres.*
Today, only the little town of San Giminiano gives an idea of the appearance of a district of Florence in the thirteenth century.

PALAZZO DAVANZATI. *This fourteenth-century private dwelling is half-way between the tower-house and the seigniorial palace; on the ground floor are the entrances to the storerooms. The loggia, added in the fifteenth century, reflects the transition to a more agreeable and serene way of life. The inner courtyard, with its play of light and shade, suggests an engraving by Piranesi. The Palazzo Davanzati is now a museum designed to illustrate a typical old Florentine dwelling.*

PALAZZO RUCELLAI. *A fifteenth-century palace designed by* LEON BATTISTA ALBERTI *(1404–1472), the great theoretician of the classical architecture of the early fifteenth century, and built by Rossellino. This admirable example of civil architecture reflects the ideas of Alberti and his search for the beautiful as an absolute value representing a pre-established harmony between Man and the universe. Unfortunately, the narrow Via della Vigna Nuova does not allow sufficient distance from which to admire*

PALAZZO DAVANZATI

PALAZZO RUCELLAI

PALAZZO BARTOLINI-SALIMBENI

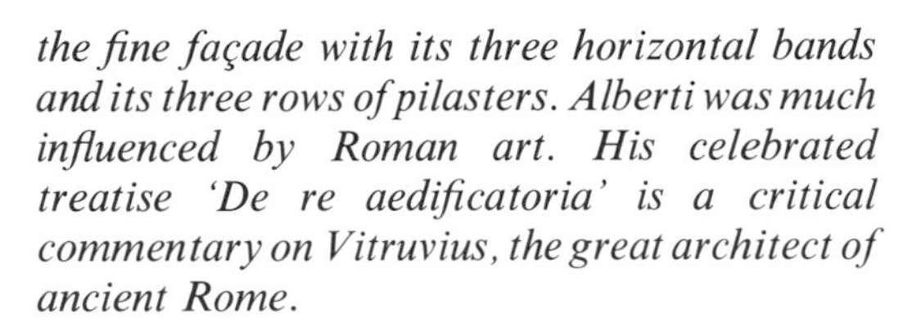

the fine façade with its three horizontal bands and its three rows of pilasters. Alberti was much influenced by Roman art. His celebrated treatise 'De re aedificatoria' is a critical commentary on Vitruvius, the great architect of ancient Rome.

PALAZZO BARTOLINI-SALIMBENI. *Built by Baccio d'Agnolo from 1517 to 1520. Its classical forms are inspired by Raphael and Roman architecture. It is an example, unique in Florence, of the light and graceful style of the latter phase of the Renaissance. Traditionally, Florentine palaces were more robust. It now accommodates the French Consulate.*

CASE DEGLI ALIGHIERI, *reconstructed in the Gothic style at the beginning of the twentieth century on the site where Dante's family resided.*

The Commune of Florence never knew the democratic régime of which Dante and Machiavelli dreamed. Before being monopolized by the Medici, the government of the city never concerned more than a hundred or so rival families who looked for support either to the Pope or to the Emperor. But in the second half of the thirteenth century an important change took place: the wealthy bourgeoisie assumed power in place of the feudal and military nobility. Shortly before the death of the Emperor Frederick II (1250), a revolt brought a new régime, the *primo popolo*. The rich merchants became the rulers of the city, supported by the craftsmen, and harsh measures were taken against the nobility. Florence now enjoyed ten years of economic and political expansion. Then in 1260 Manfred, the son of Frederick II, crushed the Florentine army at Montaperti. The Pope appealed for protection to Charles of Anjou, brother of St Louis; Charles became king of Sicily and *podestà* of Florence, bringing the city another ten years of prosperity. The *Arti Maggiori* or greater guilds – especially the richest, the *Calimala* (importers and refiners of foreign cloth), the *Arte della lana* (wool guild) and the *Arte del cambio* (banker's guild) – gradually acquired control of the councils. After the death of Charles of Anjou, the 'ordinances of justice' (1293) organized the powers of the Signoria. This was the *secondo popolo*. Seventy-three 'great and powerful' families were excluded from all participation in political life. The majority were nobles, but *magnati* who had made their fortunes in business, such as the Bardi and the Frescobaldi, were also affected. The newcomers to power were the most enterprising merchants of the *popolo grasso*, the Peruzzi, Acciaiuoli, Alberti, Strozzi, Pitti and Medici. The *Arti Maggiori* were to retain power despite the financial crises and tragic events of the fourteenth century: the Black Death of 1348, the struggle between 'Whites' and 'Blacks', and the reign of Gautier de Brienne, duke of Athens, whom the Florentines expelled four years after having invited him to be their ruler.

The popular revolt of the wool-carders, the *Ciompi*, led by Michele di Lando, resulted in the inept government of the *Arti Minori* or lesser guilds (1378–1382). Once the storm was past, however, the rich families of the wool and banking industries reassumed their prerogatives. For a time a small clique comprising Masolo degli Albizzi, Gino Capponi and Niccolò da Uzzano ruled the city, exiling families whose ambitions or wealth seemed dangerous – the Alberti, the Strozzi, and Cosimo de' Medici. The Medici finally emerged triumphant because they had succeeded in winning the support of many of these wealthy families and ruining or banishing the others, although they were never completely free from treachery.

The Florentine populace which, as Machiavelli wrote, did not have opinions but passions, was an instrument in the hands of the most skilful and powerful. To the sounds of the famous bell, the *vacca* (later removed from the Palazzo Vecchio by Cosimo I), the Signoria summoned the people in front of the palace for matters of grave importance so that a special commission, the *balia*, could be appointed. Without really playing a part, the people were thus used to ratify certain decisions. Out of the city's one hundred thousand inhabitants, only two thousand participated in political affairs, and the large majority of these were dependent on the great families. Many Florentines longed to be elected to the councils, but few showed independence or integrity when they were elected.

The activity of these rich burghers was modified by the development of commerce and the movement of capital. They were no longer merely manufacturers and merchants, but financiers and bankers. Many of them had a taste for knowledge and the arts, and there now appeared a new

type of man who, like the ancients, sought to perfect all his faculties, intellectual, moral and physical.

Pico della Mirandola, famous chiefly as a humanist, and Leon Battista Alberti, the great theoretician of architecture, were very learned and combined physical dexterity with moral strength, beauty and nobility with charm and intelligence. If they were great geniuses, the same 'perfectionist' aspirations were to be found throughout this gifted society of men.

The star of Lorenzo the Magnificent overshadowed the remarkable men who surrounded and sometimes surpassed him: Palla Strozzi was the generous patron of the arts which Lorenzo himself could never be; Giovanni Rucellai, the exemplar of the humanist great lord, asked his friend Leon Battista Alberti to draw up the plans for his palace and for the new façade which he had decided to give to Santa Maria Novella.

Santa Maria Novella, begun by the Dominicans towards the end of the thirteenth century, was the first of the great Florentine churches. Of a pure Tuscan Gothic style, it bears witness to the simplifications which the mendicant orders of Italy brought to the Cistercian Gothic architecture that had come from France. Wishing to give the nave, intended for preaching, a striking depth, the Dominican architects reduced the width of the vault from the transept, doubled the number of pillars and raised the floor on two steps, thus creating a false perspective. In the sixteenth century, alas, Vasari left his mark on the church, as he did at Santa Croce, decorating the paving of the floor and placing large stone altars of mediocre quality against the whitewashed walls. The façade of Leon Battista Alberti blends perfectly with the rest of the building; simple and harmonious in its lines, it remains faithful to the interplay of white and black marble which had been traditional in religious architecture since the Romanesque period. The main portal has a Classical sobriety. The two reversed volutes concealing the slope of the roof on each side were to play a part in the history of architecture; subsequently imitated and developed, they became one of the most original features of the façades of numerous Baroque churches.

Inside the church, a fresco by Masaccio, the *Holy Trinity* (1428), is of wonderful simplicity. The Strozzi Chapel is decorated with frescoes by Nardo and Andrea Orcagna (1328–1331) which have a deep mysticism. In the chancel, the Tornabuoni Chapel has some famous frescoes by Ghirlandaio (1485–1490) which illustrate the lives of the Virgin Mary and St John, and are among his finest works. The master worked on these frescoes with a large number of pupils, among them the young Michelangelo.

A large part of the adjacent monastery, which offered its hospitality to numerous ecclesiastical dignitaries and played an important role in the history of Florence, is now used as barracks. Fortunately, the wonderful cloisters have not been militarized. The Green Cloister, which was decorated with frescoes in two colours, green and sienna, was the work of Paolo Uccello and his pupils. Most of the frescoes, already in poor condition, were ruined by the floods of 1966; in some cases it has been possible to preserve the *sinopia*, the outlines drawn on the wall before the colours were laid on. However, two restored lunettes, *The Flood* and *The Sacrifice of Noah*, show this artist's power of foreshortening and his dramatic sense of perspective.

The Spanish Chapel, facing on to the cloister, is so named because at one time it was reserved for the noblemen of the retinue of Eleonora of Toledo, wife of Cosimo I. Built about 1340, it is covered with some delightfully coloured frescoes attributed to Andrea di Bonaiuto (fourteenth century), illustrating the Dominican faith and glorifying St Dominic and St Thomas Aquinas, the great theologian of the Order. The fresco of *The Church Militant and Triumphant* expresses vividly the missionary violence of the Dominicans: at the feet of the Pope is a herd of sheep, the faithful, guarded by two dogs, white and black, the colours of the Dominican habit; farther away, dogs are seen killing the wolves that are trying to carry off the lord's sheep (an allusion to the bloody battles which the Dominicans waged against heresy).

The disciples of St Dominic did not share the spirit of benevolence and forgiveness so dear to the followers of St Francis. They were a militant Order, ready to guarantee the triumph of the Church, whatever the cost in terms of injustice and suffering. In 1244 Piero of Verona, the first Dominican saint, had led the massacre of the *patareni* who, like the Catharians and the Albigenses, believed in the existence of a God of Good and a God of Evil, and who preached an austere morality. In the eleventh century, Florence had played an important part in the reform of the Church, with S. Giovanni Gualberto and the monks of Vallombrosa. In the thirteenth century, the activity of the mendicant orders, the Franciscans and Dominicans, had given religious life a new intensity. In the fourteenth century, however, the Church was to lose something of its power over human thought and social life. It was seriously affected by the exile of the Popes to Avignon from 1309 onwards, and then by the Great Schism and the succession of 'anti-Popes' in the latter quarter of the century. The development of commerce and wealth, and the increasing appetite for luxury and culture, compelled the Church gradually to relax its grip. Yet Burckhardt was justified in refuting the tradition which represented the Renaissance as a time of unbelief, hardly different from the eighteenth century in France: first, because a large part of the Church, led by the Franciscans, had contributed to the awakening of this new awareness of the world and its possibilities which is the hallmark of the Renaissance; and second, because religious tradition and fervour had remained strong, the discovery of Antiquity being an act of emancipation for only a limited number of privileged persons. And if even the greatest of the humanists, Poliziano, Pico della Mirandola and Marsilio Ficino, strove to broaden the religious vision of the world, they never attacked the Church directly.

The *Divine Comedy* was the epitome of the Christian world between the year 1000 and the Renaissance and a scent of profanity was already present in this poem dedicated to the glory of Thomism, which itself had opened up Christian thought to the philosophy of Antiquity. Beside Plato and Cicero, those often vaunted gods, Dante has his place in the birth of humanism, a humanism which in its form, alas, often imitated ancient models too slavishly and which in its content seemed lacking in boldness. Marsilio Ficino declared that God is the source of all light and stressed the harmony existing between Platonic philosophy and the Christian religion, which he attempted to combine in a single system. The same preoccupations with religious renewal inspired Pico della Mirandola, whose writings, intended as messages of peace and concord, were condemned by the Pope; a friend of Savonarola, Pico della Mirandola yearned for a

universal religion. 'O supreme generosity of God the Father! Supreme and wonderful happiness of Man, to whom it is granted to be what he wishes, to have what he wants.' These were the hopes cherished by the humanists; in this time of discovery when, in imitation of Antiquity, they were striving to exalt the strength and genius of Man, they wanted the Church, which had always stifled human ambition, to widen its vision and take part in this conquest. But the Church, often unjust and impure in the temporal domain, was cautious in spiritual matters and protected dogma from this adventure of the human imagination.

If, in spite of their preoccupation with the spiritual, the humanists have been accused of paganism, this is because of certain excesses, peculiar to the literary figures of the period, to which their passion for Antiquity led them. It is obvious, however, that they were saluting the ancient gods more as artists than as believers. Lorenzo the Magnificent, in his song *Bacchus and Ariadne*, proclaims his preference for the gods of bygone times, but at this same period he was writing hymns of praise to the Virgin Mary which possess a touching fervour. In this predilection for the ancient there was the artifice and affectation of a fashion reminiscent of the poets of the Pléiade in France, but without the talent of Du Bellay or Ronsard.

Between the late thirteenth and fourteenth centuries, when first Dante, then Petrarch and Boccaccio, made Tuscan the most refined literary language in Europe, and the flowering of the sixteenth century with Ariosto, Tasso and Machiavelli, the humanists represented a century lacking in invention and genius. They were paralysed by their slavish admiration of Antiquity, at the very time when artistic creation had reached the peak of its power and its glory. Nevertheless, they were the leaven which fermented the minds and hearts of the intelligentsia of the time; by encouraging the curiosity and enthusiasm of the painters, sculptors and architects, they played a decisive role. To be a humanist should have been a virtue, but it was above all a profession, with all the conventional courtesies, vanities and servilities. Knowledge intoxicated some mediocre minds and led them to blasphemy; astrology and sorcery became fashionable. By the beginning of the sixteenth century, accused of impiety and often mocked, the humanists were discredited.

If the Quattrocento remained a religious century – and it could not have been otherwise – it nevertheless saw the power of the Church become less restrictive. Religious themes continued to be the subject of most works of art, but artists treated the themes in a quite different manner. Instead of the fervour of a fresco by Giotto or a crucifix by Brunelleschi, one finds the graceful ease of Verrocchio's drawing and the elegance of Ghirlandaio's frescoes. Faith, which had been a passion, became a tradition.

SANTA MARIA NOVELLA – CRUCIFIX. BRUNELLESCHI

And although, in the first half of the Quattrocento, the example of Antiquity, and in particular the writings of Cicero, served to exalt the moral and civic virtues of the best citizens, the easier life which people now led and the greater freedom of morals gave rise to much profligacy. Savonarola's reaction against impiety and scandalous behaviour was shared by the majority of Florentines. But morality is one thing and life another. The Church had resigned itself to this fact at an early stage in its history, sometimes even turning it to advantage.

Cosimo the Elder, who often came to meditate in a private cell in the monastery of San Marco, kept concubines; a beautiful Circassian slave-girl gave him a son who made a career in banking. The monk Filippo Lippi, while painting a fresco in a convent, abducted a young nun who became the mother of Filippino Lippi. Such incidents aroused more amusement than indignation.

Even in the Middle Ages the Church, whose influence made itself felt on every aspect of social life, was by neces-

sity indulgent towards the excesses of the mighty. As for the populace, religious festivals, like carnivals, often ended in orgies. If the clergy had for a long time suppressed the ideas of Antiquity, it was for reasons of state rather than from moral indignation. Admittedly, the ancients had exalted pleasure while they themselves were speaking to men of sin and suffering, but much more dangerous to the authority of the Church was the powerful call to liberty contained in the writings of Antiquity, an idea that might encourage the emancipation of minds and consciences from the servitude in which religion held them. The Platonic message of freedom of thought and will, rediscovered by the Renaissance, was eventually to lead to the Reformation.

As far as morality is concerned, it must be emphasized that it was the seventeenth century above all which saw the emergence of that official prudery to which Florence and Italy, with hypocritical docility, were to submit their impetuous blood and their natural propensity for love.

WOODEN CRUCIFIX *by* FILIPPO BRUNELLESCHI *(1377–1446).*
THE BIRTH OF ST JOHN BAPTIST *by* DOMENICO GHIRLANDAIO *(1449–1494).*
These two works, separated by more than half a century, reveal two contrasting religious climates: on the one hand a deep fervour, and on the other an amiable indifference.

Vasari relates that, when Brunelleschi told Donatello that the figure of his Crucifix (now in Santa Croce) resembled a peasant, Donatello angrily challenged him to do better. Brunelleschi made no reply, but some time later invited Donatello to lunch in his workshop. Arriving with some eggs in his apron, Donatello was so surprised on seeing Brunelleschi's Crucifix that he let go of his apron, silent with admiration amid the broken eggs.
There is another story which is highly revealing of the intellectual character of the Quattrocento artists. One day Brunelleschi and his friends decided to talk in front of 'Il Grasso', a wood-sculptor, as if he were someone else; the game was carried on for such a long time and so cleverly that the poor man began to doubt his own identity and to wonder who he really was. Fortunately, the game was stopped when he was about to throw himself into the Arno.

The ordinary folk of Florence, though doubtless much like the people of other cities, somehow seem different to the visitor looking for characters of flesh and blood to bring to life the fascinating history of this city, to fill its streets, its churches and its palaces.
This young flower-seller might thus be Donatello's favourite pupil, or this priest oblivious of life's luxuries and vanities, an indignant 'piagnone' and fervent disciple of Savonarola – and could not this good-hearted but eloquent market-gardener suddenly become the leader of the poor, ready to attack the Signoria like Michele di Lando with his Ciompi?
As for the two young men standing beside a vendor of tripe (a dish greatly appreciated by Florentines even in the sixteenth century), they could almost be favourites of Alessandro de' Medici, first duke of Florence, whose assassination by his cousin Lorenzino in 1537 was to inspire Alfred de Musset's drama 'Lorenzaccio'.

PIZZIC

This Virgin of the Annunciation, a terracotta of the early fifteenth century, has the elegance of a noble lady of the Renaissance. The MUSEO BARDINI, *which with the* MUSEO HORNE *is one of the most interesting of the city's smaller museums, was built in 1923 by the antiquarian Stefano Bardini to house the collections which he presented to the city of Florence. It is particularly rich in statuettes and 'tondi' of the Virgin, wood-carvings and terracottas of the fifteenth and sixteenth centuries.*

A visit to the MUSEO SIEBERT *is also recommended – its collection of armour is one of the finest in the world. The* PALAZZO DAVANZATI *houses the museum of old Florentine furniture (some fine pieces from the medieval and Renaissance periods). The sumptuous apartments of the* PALAZZO CORSINI, *closed after the floods of 1966, are decorated with eighteenth-century frescoes and paintings of the sixteenth and seventeenth centuries (Pontormo, Bronzino, Parmigiano, Guerchino, Salviati, Salvatore Rosa and the Baroques). The* MUSEO ARCHEOLOGICO *possesses a rare collection of Etruscan objects which, alas, was badly damaged in the floods of 1966. Its garden is one of the most entrancing in Florence.*

p. 141
Detail from THE CHURCH MILITANT AND TRIUMPHANT, *one of the frescoes in the Spanish Chapel adjoining the main cloister of Santa Maria Novella. This painting glorifies the mission of the Dominican Order; in contrast, the artist has also depicted the pleasures and vanities of life. These frescoes, recently restored, are attributed to* ANDREA DI BUONAIUTO, *a Florentine painter influenced by Sienese art.*

Florence is the city of design and pure lines. If it left to the Venetians the privilege of being the great colourists of Italian painting, this was perhaps because it wished to remain faithful to the gentle and yet severe harmony with which it was surrounded. Its simple, restrained colours, shunning brilliant effects, reflect its intelligence.

S FRANCESCO
FIESOLE
EL PRATO
D'OGNISANTE
SLVCIA
SARDIGNA

FIORENZA

STOCK

THE HISTORY OF FLORENCE

Bronzes of the fifteenth and sixteenth centuries. From left to right: 'Orpheus' – 'Venus' – 'The Child with the Dolphin' by Verrocchio – 'Pluto' – 'Juno' by Giambologna.
Page 150 'Hercules'. Page 151 'Satyr' by Il Riccio.

I

From the Roman city to the medieval Commune

(sixth century B.C.*–twelfth century* A.D.*)*

In the sixth century B.C. the Etruscans founded Fiesole. In 59 B.C. Julius Caesar established a small colony in the valley to control the crossing of the Arno. Florence doubtless owed its Roman name, Florentia, to the season in which it was founded, the spring, the time of the *Ludi Florales*. In the first century A.D. Eastern merchants settled there, bringing with them the cult of Isis. By the end of the second century the city numbered about ten thousand inhabitants and Christianity had been introduced by Syrian traders. In the fourth century, the bishop Zanobi was contemporary with St Ambrose of Milan.

● Florence was invaded by the Ostrogoths in the fifth century and by the Lombards in the sixth; it was conquered by the Carolingians at the end of the eighth century and became a county and a diocese. In 854, Lothair I united Florence and Fiesole in a single county, the largest in Tuscany, of which Florence became the capital. The city was fortified in the tenth century to resist the Hungarian invasions. Henry II, Holy Roman Emperor, now held nearly all Italy under his sway; a friend of Hildebrand, bishop of Florence, he took an interest in the city, founding the monastery and church of San Miniato. Florence played a part in the reform of the Church in the eleventh century. S. Giovanni Gualberto founded the Order of Vallombrosa (1036); in 1055 a reforming Council brought the Pope, the Emperor Henry III, and a hundred and twenty bishops to the city, which became one of the chief centres of Christendom.

● Matilda, countess of Tuscany, supported Pope Gregory VII against the Emperor Henry IV, granting the inhabitants of Florence certain rights and privileges. After her death (1115), followed in 1125 by that of Henry V, the last emperor of the Salian dynasty, the Commune of Florence gradually assumed power. In 1125 it attacked Fiesole and destroyed the ancient city. In 1154 the imperial legate granted the Commune civil and criminal jurisdiction. In 1183 the Commune was recognized by Frederick I Barbarossa.

II

The commercial middle class takes over the government of Florence, dominates Tuscany and establishes itself in international economic life

(thirteenth and fourteenth centuries)

Since the end of the twelfth century, power had remained in the hands of the noble families, but discord among them eventually led to the adoption of rule by foreign *podestà*. This régime brought Florence twelve years of peace (1207–1220) which promoted the rapid development of commerce (expansion of trade and organization of the various merchant guilds: the *Arti Maggiori* and *Arti Minori)*. In alliance with the Pope, Florence was obliged to combat the Catharian heresy. The murder of Buondelmonte in 1215 provoked the quarrel among the nobles which was gradually to develop into the political conflict between the Guelphs, the champions of the Pope, and the Ghibellines, the supporters of the Emperor. From 1222 to 1235 Florence overwhelmed her neighbouring commercial rivals, Pisa, Pistoia and Siena. The Ghibellines supported a popular insurrection which broadened the social basis of the government. The Emperor Frederick II installed Frederick of Antioch as *podestà* and the Guelphs were sent into exile (1248).

● The merchants and artisans took advantage of a Guelph victory to rise up against the nobles and establish the *primo popolo* (1250). The great merchants who now ruled the city conducted a policy of military and commercial expansion. The gold florin was struck in 1252. The Ghibelline alliance and Manfred, bastard son of Frederick II, were victorious at Montaperti and abolished the *primo popolo* in 1260, only to be driven

from the city in 1266 by the Guelphs and Charles of Anjou, to whom the Pope had appealed for assistance; Charles of Anjou was proclaimed *podestà* for seven years. During ten years of great prosperity Florence organized her army and her commerce, and her businessmen became the most powerful in Christendom.

● The struggle between Guelphs and Ghibellines was resumed. With the support of the artisans, the burgher class strengthened its power and introduced the régime of the *secondo popolo*. In 1293 the 'ordinances of justice' removed the nobles from power, replacing them with the *Arti Maggiori* or greater guilds and organizing the Signoria and its councils. New families occupied the leading positions of the régime, which was called the *popolo grasso*. Within the triumphant Guelph party the 'Whites', advocating a policy of moderation towards the Ghibellines and Pisa, opposed the intransigence of the 'Blacks', but the latter emerged victorious in 1302 and Dante was banished.

● Threatened by the French in 1342, Florence appealed to Robert, king of Sicily, who sent Gautier de Brienne to be its governor: But in 1343 the *popolo grasso* rose in rebellion against his autocratic rule. Some great Florentine banks collapsed (1342–1346), then plague ravaged the city (1347–1348). In 1378 the *Ciompi* or wool-carders, led by Michele di Lando, revolted and assumed power together with the artisans of the lesser guilds or *Arti Minori*, but were driven out by the burghers in 1382. The commercial burgher class had finally established an oligarchic régime in which the leading families were to be the Alberti, the Ricci, the Strozzi and the Medici.

III

Florence in the time of the Medici: from Cosimo to Piero II the Unfortunate (*1421–1530*)

The new oligarchy maintained an active external policy and the conquest of Pisa in 1406 gave Florence the free access to the sea which it had needed for its commerce. Giovanni de' Medici, elected *Gonfaloniere* in 1421, enjoyed immense popularity with the masses. The Medici company which he had founded in 1397 rapidly became one of the most successful in the city. On his death in 1429, his son Cosimo revealed an equal aptitude for business affairs. But in 1433 Rinaldo degli Albizzi, alarmed by Cosimo's popularity, had him exiled for ten years. Cosimo, however, returned the following year and made himself master of the city, though without receiving any title. His great secret was never to let his power be seen. The victory of Anghiari (1440) saved Florence from the coalition of the Visconti of Milan and the king of Sicily. So that he could control the government, Cosimo created by wholly legal procedure the Council of the Hundred (1458), which was devoted to him. He died in 1464.

● His son, Piero the Gouty, followed in his footsteps, both as businessman and as political head of Florence. He died in 1469, leaving two sons, Lorenzo and Giuliano. Lorenzo, much less capable in business matters than his predecessors, enjoyed great popularity in Florence and strove gradually to establish a firm monarchic authority without modifying the outward appearances of the Republic. To control the Council of the Hundred he instituted the Grand Council. The conspiracy of the Pazzi aimed to assassinate both brothers on Easter Sunday 1478. Giuliano was killed, whereupon Lorenzo imposed his personal rule over the city. He concentrated power in two smaller councils to which he had himself elected, so that he could intervene directly in the government. Lorenzo died in 1492, having made Florence the most powerful city in Italy.

● Lorenzo's son, Piero the Unfortunate, succeeded him and inherited a difficult situation. The Medici companies were going bankrupt. As a result of his favourable attitude towards Charles VIII, king of France, who had invaded Italy, Piero was driven from the city in 1494. Savonarola instituted a theocratic Republic, but he was burned in 1498 by the very

people who had at first supported him; but the Republic survived for another fourteen years. Taking advantage of the arrival of Charles VIII, Pisa regained its independence, thereby dealing a harsh blow at the economy of Florence.

● The Medici returned to their city in 1512. One of them, Clement VII, the second Pope in the family, led them into a policy of hostility to Charles V. After the sack of Rome by the Imperials, Florence rose up in revolt to preserve its freedom and drove out the Medici (1527). Following the agreement reached with the Emperor, Clement VII launched the troops of Charles V against Florence. The city resisted for eleven months before capitulating in 1530. The free association between Florence and the Medici, which had brought them glory and prosperity, was finally broken. Henceforth, the Medici were to rule the city by coercion and with the support of foreign powers.

IV

The grand dukes of Tuscany: from the Medici to the Lorraine dynasty, Florence becomes the cultural and artistic centre of a unified Italy

(sixteenth–twentieth centuries)

By the terms of the agreement concluded by Clement VII and Charles V, the Medici returned to govern Florence. Alexander de' Medici, a cruel person, became the first duke of Tuscany and was assassinated by Lorenzino, also called Lorenzaccio, in 1537. Cosimo the Younger succeeded him and established his sway over the whole of Tuscany, which was to be ruled by a succession of Medici grand dukes, often strange figures but lacking in personality: Cosimo I (1537–1574), Francesco I (1574–1587), Ferdinando I (1587–1609), Cosimo II (1609–1621), Ferdinando II (1621–1670) and Cosimo III (1670–1722). Theirs was an authoritarian government, the councils and the *Arti* or guilds now playing only an honorary role. Commerce, industry and then banking gradually fell into stagnation. The Florentine artists had left for Rome, summoned there by the Medici Popes. In 1734 the great powers decided at Vienna that Tuscany would be taken from Giovanni Gastone de' Medici and given in compensation to Francis Stephen, duke of Lorraine, who had been compelled to cede his duchy to the dethroned king of Poland, Stanislas Leczinski, father-in-law of Louis XV.

● Francis Stephen of Lorraine resided in Vienna with his wife Maria Theresa, heiress to the imperial throne. The grand duchy of Tuscany became a satellite of the Empire. In 1735 Peter Leopold succeeded Francis Stephen and introduced far-reaching reforms in accordance with the principles of enlightened despotism. He then became Holy Roman Emperor and was succeeded by Ferdinand III, who was compelled to leave the city at the time of the French occupation in 1799. The occupation was to last, in various forms, until 1814. In 1809 Napoleon made his sister, Elisa Bonaparte, duchess of Tuscany. In 1814 Ferdinand III returned to Florence. Leopold II, grand duke since 1824, annexed the duchy of Lucca in 1847. A liberal prince, he granted the city a constitution in 1847, but had to flee in the rebellion of 1848. He returned in 1849, but the triumphant *Risorgimento* finally drove him out in 1859.

● The plebiscite of 1860 approved the annexation of the duchy to the kingdom of Piedmont-Sardinia, which was followed by annexation to the new kingdom of Italy. In 1865 Victor Emmanuel made Florence the kingdom's temporary capital, until the Italian troops had entered Rome (1870). Henceforth, Florence was no more than a provincial capital, of no great commercial or industrial importance, but the city has remained one of Italy's most lively cultural and artistic centres.

THE MEDICI

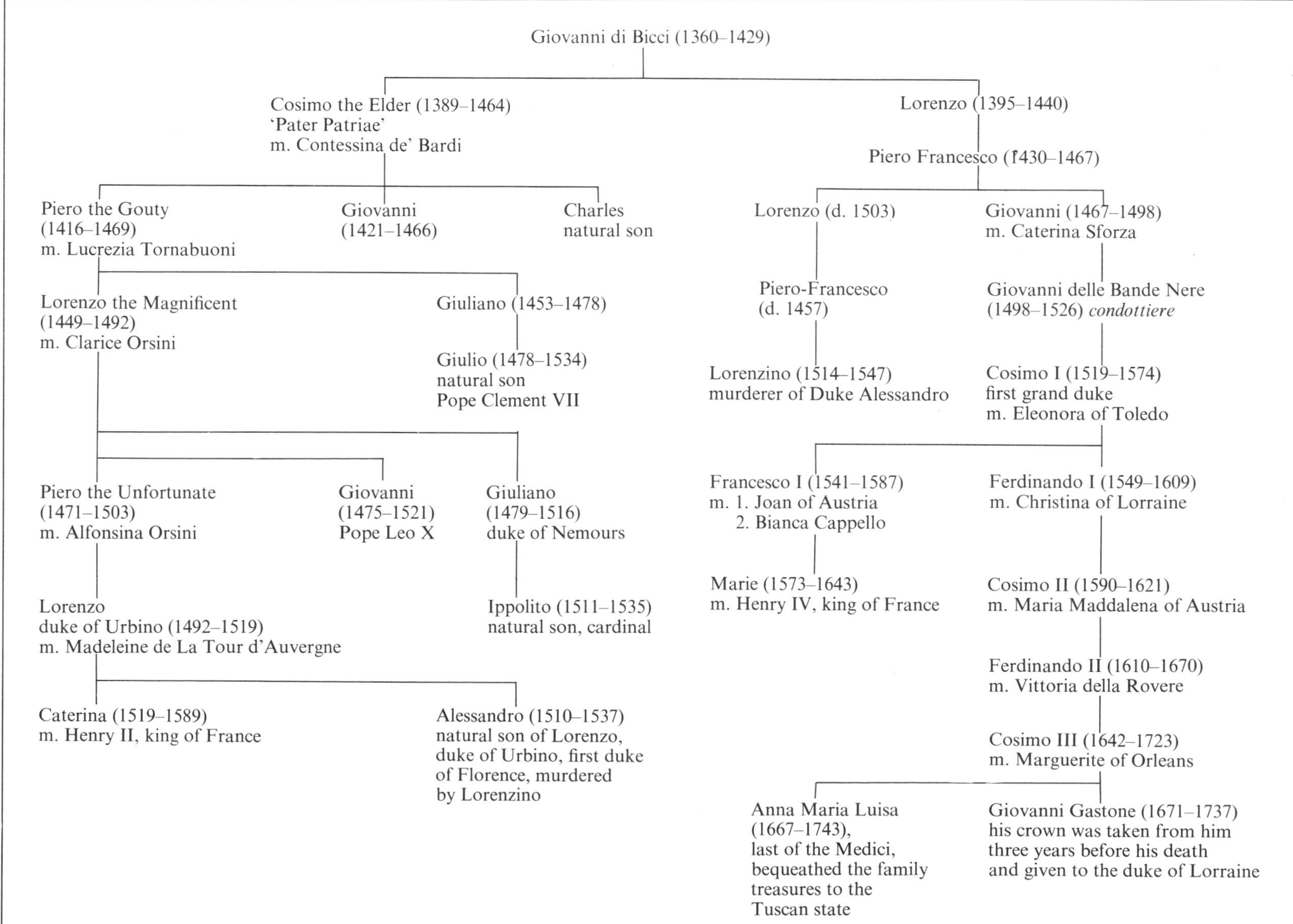

Giovanni di Bicci (1360–1429)
Cosimo the Elder (1389–1464)
'Pater Patriae'
m. Contessina de' Bardi
Lorenzo (1395–1440)
Piero Francesco (1430–1467)
Piero the Gouty
(1416–1469)
m. Lucrezia Tornabuoni
Giovanni
(1421–1466)
Charles
natural son
Lorenzo (d. 1503)
Giovanni (1467–1498)
m. Caterina Sforza
Lorenzo the Magnificent
(1449–1492)
m. Clarice Orsini
Giuliano (1453–1478)
Piero-Francesco
(d. 1457)
Giovanni delle Bande Nere
(1498–1526) *condottiere*
Giulio (1478–1534)
natural son
Pope Clement VII
Lorenzino (1514–1547)
murderer of Duke Alessandro
Cosimo I (1519–1574)
first grand duke
m. Eleonora of Toledo
Piero the Unfortunate
(1471–1503)
m. Alfonsina Orsini
Giovanni
(1475–1521)
Pope Leo X
Giuliano
(1479–1516)
duke of Nemours
Francesco I (1541–1587)
m. 1. Joan of Austria
2. Bianca Cappello
Ferdinando I (1549–1609)
m. Christina of Lorraine
Marie (1573–1643)
m. Henry IV, king of France
Lorenzo
duke of Urbino (1492–1519)
m. Madeleine de La Tour d'Auvergne
Ippolito (1511–1535)
natural son, cardinal
Cosimo II (1590–1621)
m. Maria Maddalena of Austria
Ferdinando II (1610–1670)
m. Vittoria della Rovere
Caterina (1519–1589)
m. Henry II, king of France
Alessandro (1510–1537)
natural son of Lorenzo,
duke of Urbino, first duke
of Florence, murdered
by Lorenzino
Cosimo III (1642–1723)
m. Marguerite of Orleans
Anna Maria Luisa
(1667–1743),
last of the Medici,
bequeathed the family
treasures to the
Tuscan state
Giovanni Gastone (1671–1737)
his crown was taken from him
three years before his death
and given to the duke of Lorraine

THE GREAT FLORENTINES

GIOTTO
(1266–1337)

DANTE
(1265–1321)

Dante Alighieri was born in 1265 into a distinguished Florentine family. He studied rhetoric and logic at the universities of Bologna and Padua. In 1289 he took part in the Battle of Campaldino, where the Guelphs of Florence defeated the Ghibellines of Pisa and Arezzo. He was inspired to write the poems of the *Vita Nuova* by Beatrice, the sweetheart of his childhood and adolescence, who died in 1290 and was to become the symbol of the ideal woman. Elected to the Council of Florence, he attempted to reconcile those of his party, the 'White' Guelphs, who wanted independence from Rome, with the 'Black' Guelphs. But the arrival in Florence of Charles of Valois, at the request of Pope Boniface VIII, resulted in the banishment of the 'Whites' (1301); Dante was exiled from the city and from Tuscany, under threat of burning at the stake. Exile took him to Verona, Rimini and Bologna, and he finally settled in Ravenna, where his ashes stayed after his death. His chief work, the *Commedia*, known as the *Divina Commedia* from the sixteenth century onwards, was begun in about 1309 and describes the poet's journey through Hell, Purgatory and Paradise, guided by Virgil, the symbol of the culture of Antiquity, and Beatrice, the symbol of Christian revelation. Written in Tuscan, the *Commedia* is a vast moral and political allegory, and marks the birth of Italian literature and modern poetry in general.

Giotto di Bondone was born into a peasant family in 1266 at Colle Vespignano, near Florence. A pupil of Cimabue and Cavallini, he received his artistic training from the artists of the Byzantine tradition who worked on the mosaics in the Baptistry in Florence and on those of the *Navicella* at St Peter's in Rome. In the upper church at Assisi he composed vast frescoes (1300–1310) depicting the life of St Francis. The Scrovegni Chapel on the Arena in Padua was built from Giotto's plans to serve as a framework for the great cycle of frescoes which he painted there from 1304 to 1306. The impression of strength and emotion conveyed by these paintings bears witness to the deep faith of the artist. In Florence, he decorated the Bardi and Peruzzi Chapels in the church of Santa Croce (1317–1325). He painted some pictures for King Robert of Anjou in Naples which have since disappeared, such as the Gallery of Famous Men in the Castel dell'Ovo. His popularity was immense. In 1334 the Council of Florence placed him in charge of the city's building projects. He devoted his energies chiefly to the cathedral and the Campanile until his death in 1337.

Giotto broke away from Byzantine art and the influence of Gothic expressionism by the liveliness of his faces and attitudes and by a new sense of composition. A contemporary and friend of Dante, he revealed a naturalism and an emotional power that were to be found again only a century later, in the work of Masaccio, and that were to mark all Florentine art.

PETRARCH
(1304–1374)

Petrarch (Francesco Petrarca) was born at Arezzo in 1304. His family, exiled from Florence, lived in Provence. He soon abandoned his law studies to devote himself to literature and enter holy orders. He frequented the papal court at Avignon and, impressing people with his great humanist culture and intelligence, became the protégé of the Roman family of the Colonna. At the age of twenty-three he met Laura in Avignon; she inspired in him a passionate but Platonic love which he was to express in the poems of the *Canzoniere*. In 1341 he was awarded the poet's laurel-wreath in Rome, in recognition of his researches and writings on Antiquity. He settled at Vaucluse to meditate and work, then returned finally to Italy in 1353. He retired to Arqua in 1370. Honoured in his lifetime for his work as a humanist (translations, discoveries of ancient manuscripts, poems in Latin), Petrarch is renowned chiefly for the poems of the *Canzoniere*. In these songs of despairing love, written in Tuscan, are expressed the contradictions of his personality: the longing for solitude, but also the passion for travelling and social life; the sensuality, but also the religious yearnings and the sense of the fragility of life. By casting doubts on the calm of Christian tradition, Petrarch had paved the way for the questionings of the Neo-Platonic humanists of the Quattrocento.

BOCCACCIO
(1313–1375)

Born in 1313 at Certaldo, Boccaccio spent his childhood in Florence. As a young man he was sent to Naples, where he discovered the voluptuous refinement of the court of Anjou – the meeting-place of the Italian, French, Byzantine and Arab civilizations – which was to inspire writings pervaded with the image of his beloved, Maria d'Aquino, whose praises he sang under the name of 'Fiammetta'. In 1340 he returned to Florence, where he occupied various important positions. Between 1350 and 1355 he composed his masterpiece, *The Decameron*, in which his avowed aim was to please women. The hundred tales, told by a group of young men and women who have taken refuge in a villa to escape the plague, were soon being passed by word of mouth throughout Florentine society.

His meeting with Petrarch was a decisive moment for Boccaccio. He withdrew from business affairs and turned to the wisdom of religion and humanism, writing in Latin and studying Greek. He died in 1375, a year after Petrarch.

Boccaccio, whose writing is a model of purity, gave the Tuscan language a fixed form. *The Decameron*, a highly-coloured, dramatic and, above all, satirical work, is the profane equivalent of the *Divine Comedy*. Italy had given birth to the first literary language of modern times.

BRUNELLESCHI
(1377–1446)

Filippo Brunelleschi was born in Florence in 1377. At first a goldsmith, then a sculptor, he turned to architecture only at the age of forty, after studying the art of Antiquity in Rome. Returning to Florence, he engaged in a feverish activity, won the competition held for the completion of the cathedral of Santa Maria del Fiore and, from 1420 to 1436, worked on the construction of the famous cupola which rises one hundred metres from the ground without external supports. Under the influence of the mathematician Toscanelli, he made an important contribution to the art of perspective. The elements which constitute his architectural designs are often borrowed from Rome, but are arranged in a very original manner. The Hospital of the Innocents (1420) was built to satisfy the dual requirements of urban development and perspective. The Pazzi Chapel (*c.* 1435) has a remarkably delicate grace which blends with the firm severity of the design. San Lorenzo remains Brunelleschi's most important achievement; he also prepared the plans for Santo Spirito and the Palazzo Pitti. Florence owes to Brunelleschi the style of both its religious and its civil architecture.

DONATELLO
(1386–1466)

The son of a wool-carder, Donato di Niccolò di Betto Bardi was born in Florence in 1386. He worked for a time in the workshop of Ghiberti. Doubtless assisted by his friend Brunelleschi, he mastered linear perspective and was the first to apply its principles to sculpture. He was also the first to learn how to use the rules of proportion which governed ancient art. Between the ages of twenty-five and thirty he produced his first masterpieces: *St John Baptist* for the Cathedral and the statue of *St George* for Orsanmichele. A few years later, he carved the bas-reliefs of the *Cantoria* in Santa Maria del Fiore and also the *David* for the Bargello. Called to Padua, he modelled and cast in bronze the first equestrian statue of the period, the *condottiere Gattamelata*. He then returned to Florence and carved a *Mary Magdalene* for the Baptistry and the panel of the *Deposition* for the pulpit in San Lorenzo. He died in 1466, having been paralysed for several years.

By a deep study of expression and movement, Donatello gave ancient forms an intense life. The innovating power of his art was to have a great influence on the sculptors and painters of the Quattrocento.

BOTTICELLI
(1444–1510)

Born in Florence, Botticelli became the pupil of Filippo Lippi at the age of fifteen, and also came under the influence of Verrocchio and Pollaiuolo. Around 1470 he painted his first original pictures: *Fortitude*, *Adoration of the Magi* and *Assumption of Mary*. At the request of Pope Sixtus IV, he executed several frescoes for the Sistine Chapel (1481). In Florence he worked for the Medici family, painting mythological allegories inspired by the Platonic Academy: *Spring* (1478) and *Birth of Venus* (1485). He also painted numerous religious pictures, especially of the Madonna and Child, which were often circular (*tondi*). Although full of spirit and impudence as a young man, Botticelli became a melancholy, anguished person with age. The preaching of Savonarola seems to have touched him deeply. He illustrated Dante's *Divine Comedy* with tormented drawings. Sick and forgotten, he died at the age of sixty-five. When the nineteenth century rediscovered the Florentine Quattrocento, he became its most popular artist. In his earliest works Botticelli shows a cleanness of line and a precision of form which he doubtless acquired from the goldsmiths. The gravity of the faces, the refined elegance of the attitudes and the arabesque quality of the composition combine to create the mystery of an art which either fascinates or irritates, and in which harmony suffers from the uneasy association of the pagan aestheticism fashionable at this period and the workings of a restless, mystical mind.

SAVONAROLA
(1452–1498)

Girolamo Savonarola was born at Ferrara in 1452. A zealous but austere preacher, he was little heeded at first. He became prior of San Marco in Florence in 1491 and proceeded to thrust himself on the public. He believed himself to be the chosen one of God sent to reform morals and the Church. He urged Florence to repent and warned of the imminent arrival in Italy of a modern Cyrus. Shortly afterwards, Charles VIII entered Florence at the head of a victorious army. Piero de' Medici fled and Savonarola became the city's spiritual guide for four years. He proclaimed Christ 'king of Florence' and introduced a constitution. At first Florentine society, filled with a mystical terror, bowed to his moral reforms, but public opinion was soon divided. When Charles VIII left Italy, Pope Alexander VI Borgia, who despite the attacks made against him had not hitherto dared to victimize the friend of the king of France, excommunicated Savonarola (1497). He tried to have a Council convoked; his popularity dwindled and the mob attacked the monastery of San Marco. Savonarola was condemned to death, strangled and burnt.

In attempting to place the temporal domain under the spiritual power, Savonarola embodied the final reaction of medieval scholastic thought, but he was also the friend of the humanists, and left a deep mark on the consciences of Florentines. He was to be rehabilitated by Pope Julius II.

LEONARDO DA VINCI
(1452–1519)

Leonardo da Vinci – painter, sculptor, architect, engineer and musician – led a long and adventurous life. At the age of seventeen he became the pupil of Verrocchio; his first great composition, the *Adoration of the Magi*, remained unfinished. When he was thirty years old, he left Florence and the duke of Milan, Ludovico the Moor, became his patron. The results of his studies on light and the relief of forms appear in *The Madonna of the Rocks* (1483). In 1495 he painted his famous *Last Supper* for the oratory of Santa Maria delle Grazie. In Mantua he drew the very beautiful study for a portrait of Isabella d'Este. From 1500 to 1504 he worked on the *Mona Lisa*. In Florence he painted the *St Anne* and the fine fresco that once decorated the Council Chamber of the Signoria, *The Battle of Anghiari*. In 1513 he left for Rome, where he was ill-received by Leo X. Francis I invited him to France; Leonardo left Italy in 1515 and died at Amboise in 1519.

Discoveries of pictorial technique that foreshadow Delacroix and modern painting, a prodigious gift for draughtsmanship, an all-embracing curiosity and a vivid imagination in the scientific and technical domain, combine to make this genius the symbol of the universality to which the Renaissance aspired and seem almost to justify his ambition to make Man the equal of the gods.

PICO DELLA MIRANDOLA
(1463–1494)

Pico della Mirandola was born in 1463 at the castle of Mirandola, in the duchy of Ferrara. A child prodigy, he learnt Chaldean, Arabic, Hebrew and Greek, and conceived the idea of composing a work that would gather together all the cultural traditions of past and present. In 1484 he settled in Florence, frequenting the Academy whose leading figures included Marsilio Ficino and Poliziano. In 1486 in Rome he published his nine hundred theses or *Conclusiones philosophicae, cabalisticae et theologicae*, a compendium of Latin, Arab, Platonic and Chaldean philosophy in which his intention was to show that all cultural, religious and philosophical systems converged towards Christianity. The theses were condemned by the Roman Curia (August 1487) and Pico had to take refuge in France; he was imprisoned in the castle of Vincennes, but released at the command of Charles VIII. He returned to Florence and the court of Lorenzo the Magnificent, and published *Heptaplus*, a commentary on the hidden significance of Genesis. He became the friend of Savonarola and attacked those humanists who practised astrology. He entered the Tertiary Order of the Dominicans in 1493 and died the following year at Fiesole. His life was short but devoted to intense intellectual activity; deeply religious but rejecting Catholic dogmatism, he believed that God had given Man the opportunity to decide his own destiny.

MICHELANGELO (1475–1564)

Born at Caprese, a small town in Tuscany, of an old but impoverished family, Michelangelo was apprenticed to Ghirlandaio's workshop at the age of thirteen. Noticed by Lorenzo de' Medici, he came under the influence of his humanist entourage and began to study classical models. His first major work was the *Pietà* carved for St Peter's in Rome (1498). Returning to Florence, he carved the *David* (1504) which brought him glory and which symbolized the independence of the city. In the Grand Council Chamber he painted the fresco *The Battle of Cascina*, a masterpiece representing the triumph of the nude, which has tragically been destroyed. He also painted the celebrated *tondo* of the *Holy Family*. Summoned to Rome by Pope Julius II, he worked on the ceiling of the Sistine Chapel from 1508 to 1512 and designed the Pope's tomb, a mighty project which was only completed forty years later, and even then was reduced to the two *Slaves* now in the Louvre and the *Moses* which provides the sole adornment of the tomb of Julius II in the church of St Peter's Chains in Rome. For the Medici Pope Leo X, Michelangelo prepared the plans for the façade of San Lorenzo, which he never in fact began, and those for the Laurentian Library. For Cardinal Giulo de' Medici, the future Pope Clement VII, he designed the New Sacristy of San Lorenzo and carved the two famous Medici tombs which he left unfinished in 1534. After the sack of Rome by the Imperials in 1527, Michelangelo was given the task of fortifying Florence. In 1534 he settled in Rome, painted the fresco of *The Last Judgement* in the Sistine Chapel (1536–1541) for Pope Paul III, and devoted his energies mainly to architecture (Palazzo Farnese, dome of St Peter's, Piazza del Campidoglio). When he died, his body was secretly transported to Florence. Michelangelo is undoubtedly the greatest creative force that humanity has known.

MACHIAVELLI (1469–1527)

In 1498, four years after the Medici had been banished, Machiavelli entered the service of Florence. Savonarola died that same year, but the Republic was to survive him by fourteen years during which Machiavelli constantly defended it against the ambitions of the king of France, Louis XII, and the bellicose authoritarianism of Pope Julius II. Secretary of state and travelling ambassador, he revealed the fruits of his experiences in his diplomatic reports, which foreshadowed the themes of his later political works. Suspected of having taken part in a plot against the Medici, he was arrested, tortured and banished in 1512 when the family returned to power. He sought refuge in the village of Sant'Andrea. His exile was the period of his greatest literary activity. During these years he wrote his two most important works: *The Prince*, a critical commentary on the ideology of power from ancient times, and the *Discourses on the First Ten Books of Titus Livy*; and also a play, *The Mandrake*, an essay entitled *The Art of War* and a *History of Florence* which he never completed.

Paradoxically, the writings of Machiavelli, a man of experience and moderation, a genuine democrat who analysed reality with lucidity but without enthusiasm, were to become the Bible of tyrannical monarchs.

TOURIST ITINERARIES AND SUGGESTIONS

1 PONTE VECCHIO – PIAZZALE MICHELANGELO – PIAZZA DELLA SIGNORIA – PALAZZO VECCHIO – DUOMO – BAPTISTRY – OPERA DEL DUOMO.

Morning

Allow thirty minutes to walk along the embankment (the Lungarno Corsini), see the Santa Trinità bridge, cross the Ponte Vecchio, stroll along the embankments of the Oltrarno towards the Piazza Poggi and up the slope to the Piazzale Michelangelo, where you have a marvellous panorama of the city. From there, take a taxi to the Piazza della Signoria.

If you fancy a drink of chocolate with cream, have one at *Chez Rivoire* (it is really delicious) before visiting the Piazza, the Loggia dei Lanzi, and the inner courtyard and apartments of the Palazzo Vecchio (do not miss the Room of Maps), which should take about one hour.

Lunch

Either on the Piazza della Signoria (*Cavallino*) or near the Duomo (*Gastone*, Via del Proconsole 55, or *Palazzo Antinori*, Piazza Antinori 3).

Afternoon

A visit to the Baptistry and cathedral takes about forty-five minutes. For the Museo dell'Opera del Duomo (open from 2.30 to 6 p.m.), opposite the cathedral apse, allow at least half an hour. This peaceful museum, off the main tourist routes, contains some wonderful works from the golden age of Quattrocento sculpture which absolutely must be seen.

2 SANTA CROCE – PAZZI CHAPEL – BARGELLO MUSEUM – FIESOLE.

Morning

A visit to Sante Croce takes about half an hour. Allow another half an hour for the Pazzi Chapel, one of Brunelleschi's masterpieces, and the main cloister.

A visit to the Bargello Museum (open from 10 a.m. to 4 p.m., closed Tuesdays) can take from three-quarters of an hour to two hours, depending on the individual. It contains the most famous masterpieces of Florentine sculpture of the fifteenth and sixteenth centuries (though only one work of Michelangelo), and also some fine collections of ivories, Urbino faience, ewers (twelfth-century French art) and enamels from Limoges.

Take a taxi (fifteen minutes) or a bus (from Piazza San Marco) to Fiesole. You can have lunch on the Piazza Mino da Fiesole, either at the *Pizzeria buca San Romolo* or at the more luxurious neighbouring restaurant, *Mano*.

Afternoon

Go up to the monastery of San Francesco. See the Roman theatre and the cathedral, then walk down Via Vecchia Fiesolana to San Domenico and from there on to the Badia Fiesolana. You can then either return to Florence by the San Domenico bus or, if you have a car, go to Settignano or follow some delightful little roads which lead to the villas of Petraia and Castello.

3 SANTA MARIA DEL CARMINE – SANTO SPIRITO – OLTRARNO – UFFIZI GALLERY.

Cross the Arno to visit the left bank district (the Oltrarno). Allow two hours. First see the Brancacci Chapel of the church of Santa Maria del Carmine (frescoes by Masaccio). Stroll along the lanes and see the Piazza Santo Spirito and the inside of the church, which is fairly faithful to Brunelleschi's original plans. One could spend days in this charming district, full of antique-dealers and craft shops. There are some splendid palace courtyards in Via Maggio and Borgo San Jacopo. Go to the Uffizi on foot by crossing the Ponte Vecchio.

The Uffizi is one of the most magnificent art galleries in the world. You should spend at least two hours there. A restaurant is shortly due to be opened in the Uffizi, so that visitors will be able to have lunch during their tour of the gallery.

4 SAN LORENZO – NEW SACRISTY – PALAZZO MEDICI-RICCARDI – PIAZZA SS. ANNUNZIATA – ACADEMY – SAN MARCO.

Morning

You will need about an hour and a half to visit the church of San Lorenzo (open till 12.30 p.m.), the Old Sacristy (the work of Brunelleschi and Donatello), the Laurentian Library (open 10 a.m. to 1 p.m.) adjacent to the church, and the New Sacristy with its famous Medici tombs, the work of Michelangelo (access is by a different entrance); you can then go to the neighbouring Palazzo Medici-Riccardi (9 a.m. to 1 p.m.) to see the chapel decorated by Gozzoli.

Walk to the Piazza SS. Annunziata, one of the most graceful squares in Florence. After a quick visit to the Church of SS. Annunziata, see the façade and inner courtyard of the Hospital of the Innocents (Brunelleschi). Lunch at the Pizzeria *Il Rogo*, Piazza San Marco 7r.

Afternoon

Museum of the Accademia (open from 10 a.m. to 4 p.m., closed Mondays). The famous *David* and the preliminary versions of the *Slaves* by Michelangelo (half an hour).

Monastery of San Marco (10 a.m. to 4 p.m., closed Mondays). The museum, the refectory with Sogliani's *Last Supper*, almost identical to that painted by Ghirlandaio in the church of Ognissanti (see 6) and the cells (about forty-five minutes).

Visit Orsanmichele on Via de' Calzaiuoli, both a civic and a religious edifice, decorated with statues presented by the *arti* (guilds). It contains a famous stone tabernacle. Take the lift next to the Palazzo dell'Arte della Lana to see the beautiful and tastefully restored old granary.

5 SANTA TRINITÀ – PALAZZO PITTI – BOBOLI GARDENS – THE BELVEDERE – ARCETRI AND THE HILLS OF FLORENCE – SAN MINIATO.

A short visit to Santa Trinità for Ghirlandaio's frescoes, then cross the Ponte Vecchio again and go along Via Guicciardini to the Palazzo Pitti. You will need about two hours to see the collection of paintings and the Museum of Silverware, and half an hour or more, depending on your mood, for the Boboli Gardens. You can then make for the Belvedere, where the view is superb, along the Costa San Giorgio and from there you can continue your walk, which can take two to three hours, along the delightful Via di San Leonardo. Climb up to Arcetri and, if you are a good walker, go on to the churches of Santa Margherita a Montici and San Michele a Ripaldi, two beautifully simple buildings. From there, go back down towards San Miniato along the narrow and charming Via del Giramonte.

When you reach San Miniato, the oldest, most graceful and perhaps the most moving church in Florence, you should stay at least half an hour, and if possible till sunset (open from 8 a.m. to 12.30 p.m. and from 2.30 to 6.30 p.m.).

6 PALAZZO STROZZI – PALAZZO BARTOLINI SALIMBENI – PALAZZO RUCELLAI – PIAZZA D'OGNISSANTI – SANTA MARIA NOVELLA.

Morning

As you stroll through this elegant district full of shops, from the Via de' Tornabuoni to the Piazza Ognissanti, you will see the Palazzo Strozzi, the Palazzo Bartolini Salimbeni, and the Palazzo Rucellai on Via della Vigna Nuova; then you can go into the little cloister of Ognissanti and ask to see the fresco of the *Last Supper*, undoubtedly Ghirlandaio's most sensitive and moving painting.

This walk can last an hour or two, or more if you like antique-shops (there are plenty on Via de' Fossi, but the most luxurious are on Borgo Ognissanti). You can have an excellent lunch at the restaurant *da Sostanza (Il Troia)*, Via della Porcellana 25r, but you should reserve a table beforehand.

Afternoon

You will need an hour to visit Santa Maria Novella, the cloisters and the Spanish Chapel (open till 4 p.m. and till midday on Sundays). If you have a car, you can complete your afternoon with a short trip over the hills of Chianti, through Bellosguardo, Galluzzo and Impruneta.

ADVICE

There are, of course, other churches and museums that can be visited, according to the personal tastes of the individual: the Badia (opposite the Bargello), where the church contains a fine painting by Filippino Lippi and some delicate bas-reliefs by Mino da Fiesole; the convent of Sant'Apollonia (Via San Gallo), which is decorated with paintings by Andrea di Castagno and to which you will gain admission only by perseverance; the Casa Buonarroti (beside Santa Croce), 'Michelangelo's house, which contains some small bronzes, rough sculptures and models; the minor but nonetheless interesting museums founded by antiquarians and collectors, such as the Museo Bardini (Piazza de' Mozzi), the Museo Horne (Via de' Benci 6) and the Museo Siebert (Via Siebert 26), which is famous for its collection of armour; the Museo Archeologico, which possesses a large and interesting Etruscan collection; the Opificio delle Pietre Dure (Museum of Semi-Precious Stones, Via degli Alfani 78) and, of particular interest, the Palazzo Davanzati, which is the museum of old Florentine furniture.

● While a week seems the minimum for anyone who wants to get to know Florence really well, a second week is necessary if you wish to discover some of the other beauties of Tuscany (Siena, two days; San Gimignano, one day; Luca, one day; Pisa, one day).

● One problem in Florence is the days and hours of opening of the museums and churches. As some museums are state-owned or municipal, and others private, they are organized differently and the visitor should take this into account when planning his programme. The churches are open every day, usually from 7 a.m. to midday and from 3 to 7 p.m. The state museums are open from 10 a.m. to 4 p.m., Sundays and holidays 9 a.m. to 1 p.m.

As traffic conditions are very difficult in Florence, you should always go on foot; if you plan your itinerary carefully, you can avoid long distances. If you want to go out of the city and into the beautiful hills that surround it, take your car, a taxi or one of the buses that go to Fiesole, Settignano and Impruneta.

● Remember that the cathedral, the Duomo and Santa Maria del Fiore are three names for the same building. The Oltrarno is the left-bank district of Florence, where the ordinary folk and the craftsmen's shops are to be found, though it boasts the Palazzo Pitti and many noble residences of the fifteenth, sixteenth and seventeenth centuries. Remember also that 'Quattrocento' means the fifteenth and not the fourteenth century (i.e. the 1400s).

● One of the great joys of Florence is strolling round the city. Unfortunately, the traffic is heavy and the pavements often very narrow. But in the Oltrarno one can spend hours discovering the little lanes, the craftsmen's shops, the unexpected and sumptuous palace courtyards. With a smile and the eternal 'prego' ('excuse me, please', etc.), you can nearly always be sure of satisfying your curiosity.

● The numbering of houses can be puzzling to anyone not familiar with the system. There are usually numbers in two colours, black and red, which do not follow one another even if the buildings are adjacent; the red numbers (indicated in addresses by the letter 'r' following the number) are reserved for commercial premises, the black for private houses.

● A few Florentine words and phrases: 'bischero' means 'idiot', 'imbecile' (from the name of a family in which this malady was common); in Florence one does not say 'che cosa vuoi?' ('what do you want?'), but 'e che tu vuoi?' and instead of 'vado' ('I am going') one says 'vo'; also, 'fo' ('I do, make') instead of 'faccio'; 'il tocco' means 'one o'clock' and 'punto' means 'nothing' or 'not at all'.

● A ride in a horse-drawn carriage is a traditional pastime with tourists, but is rather expensive. Try to fall in with Italian customs and between visits to different places call at some of the city's bars, which are always light, elegant and clean; after some of their marvellous coffee and tasty sandwiches, or perhaps one of their superb ices, you will set off again with renewed vigour.

● Finally, remember that, as Stendhal might have said, 'The keenest artistic emotions are at the mercy of uncomfortable shoes.'

SOME ADVICE FROM FLORENTINES

PIERO BARGELLINI

Piero Bargellini, senator of the Italian Republic and former mayor of Florence, devoted his energies after the last war to the restoration of the city's artistic monuments. He has written much about Florence and has an excellent knowledge of its history. He is the author, among other things, of a useful guide-book to the city.

The seasons and the festivals

If one is free to choose a date for a holiday in Florence, the months of May, September and October are ideal, for at these times the light and the colours are at their best. The principal festivals are:

Lo Scoppio del Carro ('The Bursting of the Cart'), Piazza del Duomo. On Easter Sunday morning, a rocket in the shape of a dove is fired along a wire from the high altar of the cathedral. The rocket is lit with a sacred flint brought back to Florence by the crusader Pazzino de' Pazzi; the flint, which is supposed to have come from the Holy Sepulchre, is kept at SS. Apostoli, a modest but graceful little Romanesque church. If the rocket reaches its target – a mass of fireworks fixed to a cart of carved wood drawn by two white oxen – and sets off the fireworks, it is an omen for a good harvest.

La Festa del Grillo ('The Festival of the Cricket'). Traditionally on Ascension Day the Florentines buy crickets in little cages and their chirping can be heard all over the city. This may be a survival of the wholesale slaughter practised in ancient times to destroy the insects which damaged crops.

Il Maggio Musicale. In May, June and July, artists of international repute come to Florence to perform at the Teatro Municipale, the Teatro della Pergola and, sometimes, in the Boboli Gardens.

Il Calcio in Costume (the costume football game). Three times a year, on the first Sunday in May and on 24th and 28th June, teams from the old quarters of Florence play on the Piazza della Signoria. This tradition, which dates from the Renaissance, was resumed in 1930. Before the game begins (it is a ball-game played with the feet and hands), the players and those taking part in the parade march through the city in period costumes. The people played *calcio* in 1530, on the Piazza Santa Croce, while Florence was being besieged by the Imperials.

La Festa di San Giovanni ('The Feast of St John'). St John is the patron saint of Florence. The fireworks display held on the evening of 24th June should be seen from Fiesole or from the banks of the Arno. In the fifteenth century the *girandole* (Catherine-wheels) were lit on the terrace of the Loggia dei Lanzi, then known as the Loggia d'Orcagna.

La Festa delle Rificolone. On the evening of 7th September, the eve of the Nativity of the Virgin, the children of the city march through the streets in a procession which ends at the Piazza SS. Annunziata. Each child carries a little light reminiscent of the paper lantern which the women from the countryside held when they came into Florence on the night of the Nativity of the Virgin.

La Mostra internazionale dell'antiquariato (the International Antiques Fair). Every two years (years ending in odd numbers), in September, Italian and European antiquarians exhibit their rarest pieces in the Palazzo Strozzi.

The Bird Fair. This is held at the Porta Romana, on the morning of one of the last Sundays in September. Birds of all species, even birds of prey, are sold.

ALESSANDRO PAZZI

A brilliant young lawyer. Like all Florentines, he adores his city and is familiar with all its amenities, including the best restaurants.

Where to stay and where to dine

The *Villa San Michele* at Fiesole is the most original and beautiful of the hotels

of Florence. Situated in an old monastery, it is tastefully furnished. Its prices are high.

The *Lungarno* hotel – Borgo San Jacopo 12 – is comfortable, modern and quiet. It looks on to the Arno.

The *Kraft* hotel – Via Solferino 2 – is modern and relatively inexpensive; it has a swimming-pool, terrace roof and open-air restaurant.

Also worth mentioning are the *Continental*, the *Ponte Vecchio*, the *Savoia* and the *Lucchesi* pension.

The good hotels in Florence are always full during the tourist season, which lasts from April to November; you should therefore book before you go.

Coco Lezzone – Via del Parioncino 26r – is a small restaurant with simple but wholesome food, typical of Florentine cuisine. Few tables and many customers.

Gastone – Via del Proconsole – is also known as *Le Mossacce* ('bad manners'); it is a tradition here for the staff to treat their customers rather rudely. You can have a quick and pleasant lunch at a reasonable price.

Buca dell'Orafo – near the Ponte Vecchio – is an attractive cellar with well prepared and tasty food. Often full.

At the restaurant of the *Palazzo Antinori* – Piazza Antinori 3 – you can have a good, quick lunch at a reasonable price.

Sostanza (Il Troia) – Via della Porcellana 25r – is of a more luxurious, international class. It is often difficult to find a table, but it is the only restaurant where you can enjoy real *bistecca alla fiorentina* (Florentine beef-steak).

Le Cave di Maiano, about seven kilometres from Florence, near Fiesole, is a country restaurant in a setting which is especially pleasant in summer. It is worth a visit for dinner.

Also to be recommended for an evening meal is the *Trattoria Omero* at Arcetri; afterwards you can take a delightful stroll. A high-quality and rather fashionable restaurant for dinner in Florence is the *Ristorante Sabatini* – Via Panzana 41–43r.

Tuscan cuisine is of a natural, peasant simplicity. Among its most typical dishes are: *crostini* (slices of toast with chicken-liver and herbs); *pappa al pomodoro* (tasty soaked bread with tomato sauce and garlic); *ribalita* (a peasant soup with cabbage, beans and bread); *fagioli all'olio* (beans in olive-oil); *bistecca alla fiorentina* (a beef-steak of a special cut and quality). For dessert, try the *zuccotto*, a recent invention (a sort of iced sponge-cake with cream and chocolate, flavoured with a liqueur). Certain dishes, such as tripe and a mixture of cockscombs, livers, hearts and pigeons' testicles, are appreciated by the Florentines but not always acceptable to foreign palates.

To complete a meal, you should order a glass of *aleatico* (a sweet wine) with some *biscottini di Prato*. Soak the biscuits in the wine, drink my health, and you will feel thoroughly satisfied.

A discerning visitor to Florence will not take coffee in a restaurant or breakfast in a hotel, but instead will go to one of the bars where the coffee is strong and the *cappuccino* (milk coffee) tasty, and where you will find simple, fragrant pastries to go with it.

Finally, you must visit *Procacci*, Via Tornabuoni 64r, to try some exquisite sandwiches with white truffles (*panini tartufati*) and a glass of white wine.

There are many excellent ice-cream shops (*gelateria*). The most famous are *Vivoli*, Via delle Stinche, and *Cavini*, Piazza delle Cure.

EMILY RAWLENCE

Born in Oxford. For four years has been studying political sciences in Florence, a city which she adores and which, like many Anglo-Saxons, she has adopted as her second home.

Living economically in Florence

There are plenty of boarding-houses or 'pensions' (*pensioni*) in Florence. I can recommend three comfortable ones for those who, by choice or necessity, do not wish to stay at any of the large hotels. There is no need to have either of the main meals, or you can have only one.

The *Monna Lisa* – Borgo Pinti 27 – quiet, central, with old-fashioned furniture and a garden.

The *Beacci Tornabuoni* – Via Tornabuoni 3 – more luxurious.

The *Bartolini* – very dignified, old-fashioned and comfortable.

If you want to be outside Florence (about fifteen minutes away), I suggest the little *Gli Olmi*, beside an olive-plantation. The atmosphere is simple and hospitable, the view splendid.

The *Morondi* is modest and is frequented by foreign girls; it faces on to Piazza SS. Annunziata, one of the finest squares in Florence.

In Florence, as in all other cities, students eat at cheap restaurants. Here are two:

Chez Nello – Borgo Tezolaio 21 (near Santo Spirito) – left-wing clientele.

Da Uccellone – Via Palmeri 37 (near Santa Croce) – a tiny room. In the summer months the proprietor puts tables on the adjacent square.

I can also recommend *Marione* – Via della Spoda 27r (near the Palazzo Strozzi) – and *La Trattoria del Carmine* – Piazza del Carmine, Oltrarno.

In the afternoon the young people of Florence often go for a walk in the countryside, which is so near and so beautiful. At Sant'Andrea, opposite the house of Machiavelli, which is open to the public, a fine old building houses the *Taverna Machiavelli*. Here you can have a raw ham sandwich or a *fettunta* (toast soaked in olive-oil and seasoned with garlic), which is delicious with a glass of Chianti.

Night-clubs for young people appear and disappear according to the latest fashion. At *Mach 2* – Via Torta 4r – there is loud music, subdued lighting and generally a distinctly 'pop' atmosphere.

The *Otto Club Discotheque* – Via Sassetti 5r – is quieter. There is no dancing at the *Gala Piano Bar* – Via dei Pandolfi 34 – but it is a pleasant place for a drink. The only restaurant in Florence open all night is *La Bussola* – Via Porta Rossa 58r.

GOGHI FAGGIONI
A talented painter and a man of culture, Goghi Faggioni divides his life between Genoa and Florence, where he lives in the Oltrarno, in an old house on the Via Guicciardini.

The seasons, lights and colours of Florence

The Tuscan countryside becomes sweet and tender at the beginning of March. In April, the spring arrives with a vengeance in an explosion of scents and colours. In May, the olive-plantations abound with red and mauve anemones. Then the summer comes to scorch both town and countryside. The autumn is also a beautiful season in Florence. The days are shorter but the weather is nearly always marvellous, and the parched land assumes a gentler aspect. Winter endows Florence and Tuscany with a mysterious charm. You should go up to Fiesole early on a misty morning. In the valley the city is invisible. Only a villa and a few cypresses emerge from the mist, or sometimes the towers, domes and church-steeples of Florence appear in the distance, shining in the light.

It is delightful to wander through the lanes of Florence, especially in the Oltrarno; to see a young father standing in his doorway and rocking his new-born child in his arms; to meet a picturesque umbrella-repairer; or suddenly to come across a vehement discussion being carried on by the old men who spend part of the day sitting on the stone ledge that runs along the bottom of the palace walls. Don't miss the beautiful stone shields with the armorial bearings of the owners, at the corners of the old palace, and the innumerable images of the Madonna and of saints which decorate the ancient walls.

I can also recommend the view of the rooftops of Florence from the top of Orsanmichele or the Bargello. Neighbours chat with one another, the women wash and hang out their linen, and on the terraces amateur gardeners tend their flowers and plants.

It is a moving experience to watch the darkness falling on the Piazza della Signoria, as one leans against the Loggia dei Lanzi or perhaps, more mundanely, sits on the terrace of *Chez Rivoire*, where the chocolate is excellent. You should also go round the parapet-walk of the Forte di Belvedere to catch the sun setting on the city, which suddenly glows in its dying rays. But it is undoubtedly on the hills of Florence, at Arcetri or Fiesole, that the greatest happiness is to be found. If you have a car, you should leave the city in the direction of the Siena road and in the late afternoon discover Certosa, Montespertoli, Certaldo, Strada in Chianti and Impruneta.

COUNTESS ALOISIA RUCELLAI
Countess Rucellai, who lives in the magnificent palace designed by Alberti, is an artist and makes beautiful jewellery in the traditional Florentine style.

Shopping

The craftsmen of Florence are proud to have been able to preserve the famous

traditions which they still follow today in creating objects of great luxury. The little shops of the goldsmiths on the Ponte Vecchio surround the statue of the most celebrated of them, Benvenuto Cellini. *Mario Buccellati*, Via Tornabuoni 69r, makes some exquisite silver pieces. *Fiaschi*, Via Guicciardini 126r, carries on another Renaissance tradition, the art of *pietre dure* or semi-precious stones, from which he carves ash-trays and some beautiful boxes. The Florentines are also great leather-workers. *Gucci*, Via Tornabuoni 73–75r, *Cellerini*, Via del Sole 9, and *Micheloni*, Borgo Ognissanti 80r, are excellent morocco-leather artists who make elegant handbags and suitcases. *Ferragamo*,

Via Tornabuoni 16r, and *Mantellassi*, Piazza della Repubblica 25r, offer elegant and comfortable handmade shoes. *Giannini*, Piazza Pitti 19, specializes in bindings. Florentine glove-making is renowned for its finesse; even gloves of peccary can be bought at very reasonable prices; two addresses are: *Barra*, Lungarno Acciaioli 2–6r, and *Nanco*, Via Tornabuoni 5. The dress-designer *Emilio Pucci* is famous among fashionable women throughout the world, but men also appreciate his neckerchiefs and ties.

There are many antique-dealers (pictures, furniture and faience) both in the Oltrarno, on Via Maggio and Borgo San Jacopo, and on the right bank, on Via de' Fossi and Via del Moro. The most luxurious are on Borgo Ognissanti.

Straw articles can be bought at *Chez Paoli*, Via della Vigna Nuova 26r. Souvenirs and small presents are available at the new market, Loggia del Porcellino. The traditional objects made in Florence, such as leather suitcases, handbags and boxes, shirts, ties, table services, straw articles, and gloves, can be found in the countless shops in the streets near the Piazza della Repubblica. The most elegant street is Via Tornabuoni, but Via Calimala and Via de' Calzaiuoli are also worth visiting.

The shops in Florence are open from 9 a.m. to 1 p.m. and from 3 or 3.30 to 5.30 or 6 p.m.

HAROLD ACTON, C.B.E.
A distinguished man of letters and collector, born of an Anglo-American family that had settled in Florence. He lives in the Villa La Pietra, which has a magnificent garden. He has written several books in which he displays a wide-ranging culture and a pungent wit: The Bourbons of Naples, Memoirs of an Aesthete, The Last Medici, *and others.*

Books to read

Those who know Italian should live the history of Florence through its great historians, Giovanni Villani, Machiavelli, Guicciardini, Varchi, Segni, and Ammirato. It is a long, complex and fascinating adventure.

In the eighteenth as in the nineteenth century, most travellers to Italy passed through Florence and many published their impressions, often repeating each other. One of the liveliest, by the Président de Brosses, was published posthumously; one of the most poetical, by William Beckford (1780–1782), expresses a proto-Romantic delight in Florentine scenery. A steady stream of English guide- and travel-books appeared after the fall of Napoleon, such as Mariana Starke's *Travels in Europe*, Lady Morgan's once popular *Letters* (1819–1820) and Lady Blessington's rather gushing *The Idler in Italy* (1823–1824). More recently, Edward Hutton has written *Florence and Northern Tuscany* and other useful guides, and Mary McCarthy has produced her highly individual and provocative *The Stones of Florence* with excellent illustrations.

As far as the civilization and art of the Renaissance are concerned, Jacob Burckhardt's *The Civilization of the Renaissance in Italy* (1867) is the first comprehensive survey of its kind and it remains a work of fundamental importance. This should be supplemented by Walter Pater's essays (1873, but constantly reprinted). Bernard Berenson's *Florentine Painters of the Renaissance* (1896) still affords a brilliant yet succinct introduction to the subject.

Giorgio Vasari (1511–1574), official painter to the Grand Duke Cosimo I, is our chief source of information about the lives of the great Florentine painters, which he recorded in a pleasant style with copious anecdotes and technical comments. Benvenuto Cellini's autobiography, well translated by J. A. Symonds, reveals not only the swashbuckling character of this superb sculptor-goldsmith but also the keen atmosphere of sixteenth-century Florence.

André Chastel is the leading French authority on the subject and there are too many German specialists to mention here. Rudolf Wittkower s *Architectural Principles in the Age of Humanism* (1962) and Erwin Panofsky's *Renaissance and Renascences in Western Art* (1960) are essential for the serious student. On Michelangelo, Professors Charles de Tolnay and Frederick Hartt, whose works are available in English, are the outstanding authorities; Lord Clark's study of Leonardo da Vinci is both learned and intensely readable; Sir John Pope-Hennessy's comprehensive volumes on Italian Gothic and Renaissance sculpture and *The Portrait in the Renaissance* are illuminating and enjoyable. Eve Borsook's *Companion Guide to Florence* and Dr Bruno Molajoli's *Florence* (in English) are among the best of recent guides.

Colonel G. F. Young's *The Medici* (1910) for all its short-comings has not yet been superseded in English; in France Marcel Brion has produced a finely illustrated book on the subject. Ferdinand Schevill's *Mediaeval and Renaissance Florence* (1936) is a standard work.

For readers of Italian, Emilio Cecchi's *Firenze* is a minor classic. Aldo Palazzeschi's *Sorelle Materassi* and *Stampe dell'800* are the most delighful of recent works of fiction, while the novels of Vasco Pratolini portray the lives of the poor with crude realism and compassion.

Dante's *Divine Comedy* is altogether too large a subject for mention here. Above all other poets he has expressed the spirit of old Florence. In him, as Richard Garnett wrote, the Middle Age lives as it does in its cathedrals; and when the cathedrals have crumbled, the *Divine Comedy* will be as fresh as it is now.

CONTENTS

1st DAY

2nd DAY

3rd DAY

4th DAY

5th DAY

6th DAY

THE PRINCIPAL MONUMENTS OF FLORENCE IN THE ORDER OF THE ITINERARY

1 Ponte Vecchio
2 Piazza della Signoria
3 Duomo and Baptistry
4 Santa Croce
5 Bargello
6 Santa Maria del Carmine
7 Santo Spirito
8 Uffizi Gallery
9 San Lorenzo
10 Palazzo Medici-Riccardi
11 Piazza SS. Annunziata
12 San Marco
13 Orsanmichele
14 Palazzo Pitti
15 San Miniato
16 Palazzo Strozzi
17 Santa Maria Novella

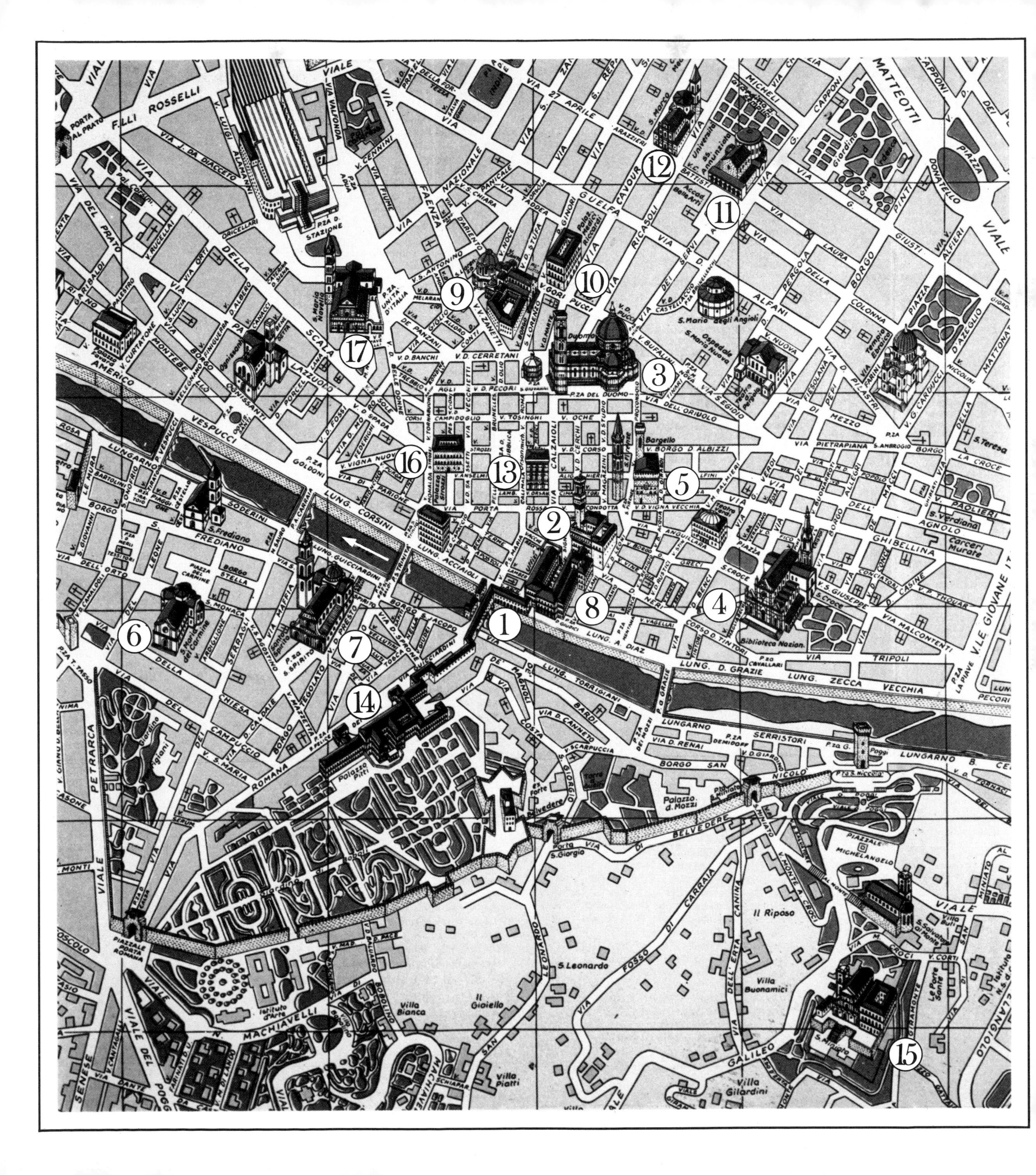

1
2
3
4
5
6
7
8
9
10
11
12
13
14
15
16
17
Duomo
Bargello
Biblioteca Nazion.
S. Frediano
S. Maria del Carmine
Palazzo Pitti
Palazzo d. Mozzi
S. Maria degli Angioli
Ospedale S. Maria Nuova
Carceri Murate
S. Teresa
S. Verdiana
Il Riposo
S. Leonardo
Villa Buonamici
Villa Bianca
Il Gioiello
Villa Piatti
Villa Gilardini
Istituto d'Arte
Piazzale Michelangelo
Piazzale Porta Romana
Porta S. Giorgio
Belvedere
LUNGARNO
LUNG. CORSINI
LUNG. ACCIAIOLI
LUNG. GUICCIARDINI
LUNG. A DIAZ
LUNG. D. GRAZIE
LUNG. ZECCA VECCHIA
LUNG. TORRIGIANI
LUNGARNO SERRISTORI
VIA TRIPOLI
VIA PIETRAPIANA
VIA GHIBELLINA
VIA FAENZA
VIA NAZIONALE
VIA CAVOUR
VIA RICASOLI
VIA GUELFA
VIA ALFANI
VIA DELLA COLONNA
VIA PINTI
VIA MATTEOTTI
VIA SCALA
VIA DELLA CHIESA
VIA ROMANA
VIA MAGGIO
VIA DE' BARDI
VIA DI BELVEDERE
VIA S. LEONARDO
VIA DI S. MINIATO
VIALE MACHIAVELLI
VIALE N. MACHIAVELLI
VIALE GALILEO
VIALE PETRARCA
VIA SENESE
VIA FOSSO DI CARRAIA
BORGO SAN NICOLÒ
BORGO PINTI
BORGO S. JACOPO
BORGO S. FREDIANO
BORGO OGNISSANTI
BORGO D. ALBIZZI
BORGO DEGLI ALBIZZI
BORGO S. CROCE
PIAZZA DONATELLO
P.ZA DEL DUOMO
STAZIONE
VIA F.LLI ROSSELLI
VIA AMERICO VESPUCCI
VIA CALZAIOLI
VIA PORTA ROSSA
VIA D. CERRETANI
VIA D. PECORI
V. TOSINGHI
VIA DELL'ORIUOLO
VIA S. EGIDIO
VIA D. BENCI
VIA MALCONTENTI
V.LE GIOVANE ITALIA
VIA DEI SERRAGLI
VIA DEL CAMPUCCIO

● *This volume was written and produced by André Barret, with the assistance of Michèle Rougé who was responsible for the layout. We must thank in particular Mr Raffaello Bencini, who provided us with most of the photographs which illustrate the book. La Scala supplied the colour reproductions of works of art. The following have also assisted in the illustration of the book: Wim Swaan, Fulvio Roiter, Ezio Quiresi, Gianni Berengo-Gardin, Arpad Elfer, Roloff Beny, Filippo Passigli, André Barret, Carlo Bevilacqua; and the agencies Alinari, Giraudon, Roger-Viollet, Fotocielo, Arnaud, and La Photothèque.*

First published in Great Britain by
Kaye & Ward Ltd
21 New Street, London EC2M 4NT
1973

First published in the USA by
Oxford University Press Inc.
200 Madison Avenue, New York N.Y. 10016
1973

ISBN 0 7182 1001 8 (Great Britain)
ISBN 0 19 519750 X (USA)
Library of Congress Catalog Card Number 73-85846 (USA)

Printed in Italy by
Arnoldo Mondadori Company Ltd, Milan